Reasoning About God,

Man and Evil

A Dialogue in *Christian Apologetics*

Magnus Nick Keehus

Joy Publishing
P.O. Box 9901
Fountain Valley, CA 92708

Theologians generally are delighted with the proof that the universe had a beginning, but astronomers are curiously upset. It turns out that the scientist behaves the way the rest of us do when our beliefs are in conflict with the evidence.[*]

Robert Jastrow

Reasoning About God, Man and Evil

A Dialogue in *Christian Apologetics*

Magnus Nick Keehus

© 1997 Magnus Nick Keehus

Printed in the United States of America

ISBN 0-939513-95-1

Published by: *Joy Publishing*
P.O. Box 9901
Fountain Valley, CA 92708

---

[*] Jastrow, Robert, *God and the Astronomers*. (W. W. Norton & Co., New York, 1978), pg. 16

To the One in whose mind I existed not only in thought eternal but also as a completed work of clay before being made.

To my dear wife and children for their patience with regards to the seemingly endless hours spent at my desk, not in just writing this book, but in various projects.

To my beloved mother who just accepted the One in whom we live and move and have our being.

To my sharp biblical mentor, Christly example of a tough-minded, yet gentle spirit of a pastor/teacher Chuck Smith—thank you for all your input and encouragement and for always being so open.

I also thank my wonderful instructor and father in the Lord — Carl Westerlund for always believing in my work.

Many thanks to my cross-country mentor philosopher and theologian William Lane Craig whose mind has taught me many things.

Also, thanks to Sally, the day and night secretary of all.

Thanks to Craig, Kent, Paul, Tom, Carl, Ray, John and Ron for reviewing the manuscript and making helpful suggestions.

And finally, to my supportive and diligent students, and Swedish brothers and sisters.

Introduction

This book was designed to stimulate the minds of those who are interested in ultimate issues. It is primarily an introductory work in support of *theism* with highlights of Christian theism. I am addressing thee main topics: (I) *Arguments For the Existence and Personhood of God*; (II) *The Folly of Man, Diversion, Radical Skepticism, Knowledge Relativism and Moral Relativism*; and (III) *God and the Problem(s) of Evil.*

Also, this book aims to communicate *philosophical truths, logic, theology* and *science* by means of a *dialogue* between an agnostic sociologist and a philosophical apologist, both of whom are graduate students in their respective fields. This format will most likely ease the task for the reader to understand the content if newly exposed to such material. Some issues may be a bit challenging for the new reader, hence, in the footnotes; various definitions can be found that clarifies certain "household words" within philosophical and apologetic circles.

There are many apologetic works far more exhaustive than this one that the reader can consult. The purpose of this work is to familiarize the *believer* and the *seeker* to the world of apologetics by means of a brief dialogue on crucial topics. Although, much more could be said concerning each argument, in limiting these subjects by not covering *everything* that could be said, one always takes the risk of committing certain generalizations, etc. But hopefully, in the scope of the whole—the totality of the content—great truths will be discovered having eternal value.

Table of Contents

Without grace,

my relationship with God is never an established

reality

and it is impossible to enjoy peace.

If my relationship with God depended on how I felt

or how I was living or on my own righteousness,

I would not be able to relate to God most of the time.

When my relationship with God

is predicated upon God's grace toward me,

however, the door of blessing is never closed.

God's blessings are bestowed on the basis of His grace,

His unmerited favor.

I *never* deserve or earn a blessing.

The blessings that come in my life are always predicated

upon God's unmerited favor to me.

God loves me so much, He blesses me anyway.

God is so good!

The truest praise is that which rises spontaneously

from our hearts as we recognize God's marvelous grace

toward us.[*]

Chuck Smith

---

[*] Smith, Chuck, *Why Grace Changes Everything* (Eugene, OR: Harvest House Publishers, 1994), pg. 37.

In the Courtyard at UCLA

Chapter One

If God Does Not Exist, Then When We Die Most Likely NOTHINGNESS Follows. But If God Does Exist, Then Most Assuredly Everlasting Happiness Ensues. Granting, Of Course, That We Respond To The Designer's Loving CALL.

Can the question of God's existence be addressed reasonably? I think so. It is, of course, an issue many choose not to pursue in our sophisticated diverted society due to their daily activities and duties, and thus it is argued that one does not simply have time for such ponderance. This is indeed the height of folly. To not think carefully and critically about this particular issue, which could have such radical eternal consequences, is indeed the ultimate example of human lunacy. This book is a fictional dialogue with overtones of real life events. *Benjamin* is a believing philosophical theist and *Sixten* an agnostic graduate student in sociology. Both are graduate students in their fields. Prior to them going their separate ways, they met in an undergraduate philosophy class at Harvard University. Ever since, they've been great friends and able to talk about everything. This takes us to a summer afternoon in the courtyard at the University of Los Angeles, California.

BENJAMIN: How have you been my friend? It's been so long since we graduated from Harvard. How's the life at Yale?

SIXTEN: Just fine, thank you! I am really enjoying their program in sociology. Now, I thought you were going to study at Oxford, but rumors hold that you are presently at Notre Dame, under Professor Alvin Plantinga. Is this really so?

B: That is correct. You see, soon after you left Massachusetts, I went to visit my younger brother in Los Angeles. The same evening I arrived he invited me to attend a lecture at Whittier College given by Plantinga, the topic was "An Evolutionary Argument Against Naturalism."[1] Back then, being the evolutionist that I was, he greatly challenged my entire worldview,[2] and after looking into his work more closely, to make a long story short, I accepted the Christian worldview as the only tenable one, and received Jesus Christ as my Savior. Shortly thereafter, I moved to Indiana to attend the University of Notre Dame, and I love it.

S: You? Have you become a theist?[3] Oh my goodness, that is one thing I could never picture you ever becoming. You were always into

---

[1]*Naturalism* holds that the universe is eternal, self-sustaining and thus without a God. The cosmos consists of matter and energy.

[2]A *worldview* is a philosophy of life concerning ultimate issues.

[3]*Theism* is the belief in an *eternal* and *personal* God who transcends the universe and possesses such attributes as *omnipotence, omniscience, omnipresence* and *self-existence*, etc.

arguing with the Christians while at Harvard, and now you have become one of them?

B: It is true that I used to be hostile towards religion. But I think I was a bit mistaken in thinking they lacked evidence for their belief, especially after attending the lecture at Whittier. I mean, this philosopher, he sort of assumed my worldview for a moment and simply pointed out that evolution, among other things, cannot produce true belief. This really bothered me since I have always been interested in truth claims.

S: So what brings you to UCLA?

B: I just visited the philosophy department. I'm considering their doctoral program in Analytical Philosophy.

S: But what about Notre Dame?

B: Well, I am going to finish my Masters of Arts in philosophy under Plantinga, but I am not sure if I want my doctorate from the same school. I'd really like to do a post-doctorate at Notre Dame. I am also considering the University of Lund, Sweden.

S: I see.

B: What are you doing here?

S: I was actually just visiting a former professor of mine that use to teach sociology at Harvard. But I am curious, what is this thing about you now being a Christian? Tell me about it.

B: As I said earlier, I think there is a great deal of evidence for the truthfulness of the Christian faith, and this is where it all begun. I was challenged on my evolutionary and atheistic beliefs and decided to check into the claims of Christianity and found them very convincing.

S: So what are you saying? Are you saying that there is sufficient evidence for Christian theism?

B: I would say so. It is at least a plausible system of thought; although, it is more than that, it is also a relationship.

S: But one cannot prove religious claims. Are you not failing to distinguish between matters of faith and fact?

B: Well, I am of the view that one can prove some things, but not all things. This is also known as critical rationalism, which you probably recall us studying when we took Philosophy of Religion at Harvard.

S: Yes, that was the view somewhere between strong rationalism[4] and fideism[5], right?

B: Exactly. The truth lies somewhere in the middle of two extremes. At least it's a guarded[6] position.

S: Well, being the truth seekers that we are, I must tell you, I am familiar with some of the arguments for the existence of God, but I am not sure whether they are totally convincing.

B: What is totally convincing anyway?

S: Well, Paul Edwards, in the Encyclopedia of Philosophy, lays out the various arguments as posed by traditional theists but there seems to be some sort of problem with all of them.

B: I think the same is true of most arguments in both camps whether one examines atheism or theism. What I have come to discover, though, is that theism has a high degree of plausibility[7]

---

[4] Strong rationalism holds that religions must be proven to be true before they are adopted as belief systems.

[5] Fideism is the view that religious systems of thought should not be rationally evaluated or criticized. It is a "faith-ism" approach to religion.

[6] *Guarding* entails the weakening of claims in order to diminish possible attacks.

[7] By plausible I mean *trustworthy* or *seemingly true*.

and explanatory[8] power. In other words, I think it is the most maintainable system of thought.

S: All right then! I am ready to dialogue. But if you want me to surrender, as one of us would always do in the past if we lost the argument, I want to see some good convincing proof.

B: Well, I cannot prove all things as I said earlier, but if you are willing to pursue what I think is the greatest ultimate question, let us hammer it out.

S: I agree, the issue ought to be pursued. Was it not Will Durant who said, "The greatest question of our time is not communism versus individualism; not Europe versus America; not even the East versus West. It is whether man can live without God."[9]

B: Yes, that was Durant, and I would agree, it surely is the greatest question. The way you and me, and everybody else answer that very question will not only determine the way we

---

[8]Explanatory power according to Ravi Zacharias entails "...the collection of facts" leading "to initial postulations, from whence we device our theories, our hypothesis, and then finally delineate our "laws." United facts and integrated deductions lead to systems...Facts help build up a theory" and "provide the descriptive elements...through which we view the world." From: *A shattered Visage: The Real Face of Atheism* (Grand Rapids, MI: Baker Books, 1990), pg.190.
[9]Ibid. p.10

live our lives, but also the way we view our entire destiny.

S: I guess you are right. Even the Oxford atheist, J.L. Mackie says,

> It is my view that the question whether there is or is not a god can and should be discussed rationally and reasonably, and that such discussion can be rewarding, in that it can yield definite results. This is a genuine, meaningful question, and an important one—too important for us to take sides about it casually or arbitrarily...the issue is not so obscure that relevant considerations of argument and evidence cannot be brought to bear upon it.[10]

S: I tell you what, why don't we go down to the Java House, and the coffee is on me. They've got these really outlandish blended mochas with ice and cream on the top and all, you will love them. How about it?

B: Hey, being the coffee addict that I am, how can I resist.

At Java House:

---

[10] Mackie, J.L. *The Miracle of Theism* (Oxford: Clarendon Press, 1982), pg. 1.

S: So tell me, what is one of the most convincing arguments you have come across thus far?

B: One of my favorites is known as the *Kalam*[11] Cosmological Argument. It has its origin in early Christian apologetics[12] and was developed by some Arabic thinkers about a thousand years ago. It was a philosophical defense for a finite view of the cosmos, or the beginning of the universe, in contrast to Aristotle's infinite assessment of the world.

S: Did you say *kalam*?

B: Yes. Are you familiar with the argument?

S: Not in detail. But I can recall a Christian philosopher by the name of William Lane Craig defending it.

B: Oh yes, Dr. Craig is the greatest contemporary defender of this argument. And what is so remarkable with Craig's defense is that he argues from contemporary "big bang"

---

[11]*Kalam* means "lit. speech', or dialectic'; applied to theology which is the 'study of divine speech'. see Glasse, Cyril. *The Concise Encyclopedia of Islam* (San Francisco: Harper & Row, Publishers, Inc., 1989), pg. 216

[12] *Apologetics* derives from the Greek word "apologia" meaning a "defense" or rational or reasonable "answer." The apostle Peter says, "Be ready *always* to give an answer [an apologia] to everyone who asks you a reason for the hope that is in you" (1 Peter. 3:15).

cosmology[13], and also greatly strengthens it philosophically.

S: Show me the form of the argument?[14]

B: It goes something like this,

   (1) Anything that begins to exist has a cause for its existence
   (2) The universe is a thing that came into existence
   (3) Therefore the universe has a cause for its existence

S: Okay, so it is a valid argument,[15] but validity does not mean that it is sound.[16] You'll have to do better than that.

B: Well, the causal principle or the law of cause and effect holds that *every effect has a cause*, and therefore supports the major premise *anything that begins to exist has a cause for its existence*.

*the universe was birthed
Thats all That's
important*

---

[13]*The Big Bang Theory* is the view that the universe came into being as a result of an explosion. *15-20 B years ago !!*

[14]By *argument* I mean a number of reasons (or premises) given to adopt the conclusion following from those reasons.

[15]A *valid* argument is where the conclusion follows from the premises

[16]A *sound* argument consists of *true* premises and a following conclusion

S: For that to be true the universe would have to be an effect.

B: Right! If we use the term *effect* rather than *begins to exist*, the argument would be as the following,

a valid argument ✓

(1) Every effect has a cause
(2) The universe is an effect
(3) Hence the universe has a cause

S: Go on.

B: If we grant validity to the big bang model and laws of thermodynamics, you know, the universe being the result of an explosion and progressing towards decay, and since energy is not being created and thus becoming thinner as it is spreading out due to the expansion of the universe, the universe certainly appears to be finite and thus is the effect of something else.

S: I am following you.

B: Astronomers maintain that planets and stars in the universe are moving away from the earth at rapid speeds, and if it was possible to rewind the motions of these planets, it would all have to have begun by one great explosion. And if the universe *began* to exist or *came into being* as a result of this explosion, well then it had a beginning point and is thus finite.

S: So if there was a beginning, there must also be a Beginner or God, right?

B: Yes, some personal agent of some sort.

S: Is it not arguable to say that this phenomenon has been going on for infinity.

B: If I am not mistaken, Einstein tried a similar argument and failed. But since the second law of thermodynamics asserts that the universe is moving towards decay or heat death, if you are correct, the universe would have to have burned up an infinity ago, which is absurd because the universe is still here.

S: Fair enough. But quantum physics has suggested that there are effects without causes. So, perhaps the universe is an effect without a cause.

B: I don't think that is very likely at all. You see, subatomic physics proposes that electrons can pass in and out of existence without any trace of a cause.[17] But the problem here is that for this to occur, a universe is needed in the *first* place, and in addition, vacuums within it. Some have also argued that although "the causal principle operates at the supraatomic level, the principle is inapplicable at the subatomic, and hence not universally true."[18]

S: I see.

B: Quentin Smith, the British atheist, also has something interesting to say regarding quantum mechanical laws. He maintains that they "state nothing about the causality or acausality of absolute beginnings, of beginnings of the existence of particles."[19] Philosopher J.P Moreland makes the following remarks,

> First, not all philosophers and physicists are agreed as to how to interpret quantum mechanics... Second, even if one interprets quantum mechanics along realist lines (quantum theory states, at least approximately, the way the world is), it does not follow that events above the subatomic level do not have

[17]Peterson, Hasker, Reichenbach and Basinger. *Reason & Religious Belief: An Introduction to the Philosophy of Religion.* (New York; Oxford: Oxford University Press, 1991), pg. 75.

[18]*Ibid.* p.75

[19]British Journal of Philosophy of Science 44 (1993), pg. 624.

causes. Even if one grants that a photon of light can pop into existence from a "quantum ghost" (sheer nothingness, which underlies every thing), it does not follow that the first event did not need a cause. Even if one can make statements like the one about quantum ghosts intelligible, and I personally doubt this is possible, macroevents still have causes. When an apple falls something caused it. It is an unwarranted extrapolation to argue from the microlevel to the macrolevel.[20]

S: Is that the only support of the argument?

B: No, there is more. Shall we continue?

S: Sure, this is getting quite interesting. But first I need a refill, I feel like my head is ready to explode, can I get you some more coffee?

B: I'll pass, thank you anyway.

S: Please, go on.

---

[20]Moreland, J.P. *Scaling The Secular City* (Grand Rapids, MI: Baker Book House, 1987), pp. 38-39.

B: All right. As we saw, some hold that the principle does not apply at the subatomic level, only at the supraatomic plain and thus, not universally true. Now, that may very well be the case, but the most important point with regards to the quantum objection is that philosophers and theologians alike point out that "it might not affect the *kalam* argument in that quantum theory does not hold that electrons appear *de novo;* matter and energy are not continually being created out of nothing, which is what the first premise asserts."[21]

S: I can grasp that.

B: So, since traditional theism affirms that the universe was created out of nothing *ex nihilo* (As Aquinas said, *"ex nihilo nihil fit"* out of nothing nothing comes) by a personal agent we call God, the quantum argument falls short since it does not pertain to *kalam*.

S: As in *agent causation*?

B: Right, a personal being or agent *caused* the universe. In addition, philosophers have argued that the notion of causality is intuitively true[22]or true by intuition. I mean, after all, if the

---

[21]Peterson, *Reason & religious Belief.* pg.75
[22]*Ibid.*

principle of causality were not true or reliable, then scientists would constantly run into contradictions while relying on this law in their explorations, but they don't.

S: Well that seems to lend at least *some* credibility to the major premise.

B: I am glad that you said that. Thus far, we have seen that the major premise of this version of the cosmological argument seems to square with Newton's law of cause and effect, while big bang cosmology actually affirms both of the premises.

S: Please, summarize the proof.

B: First, I said that the big bang seems to indicate that the universe is an effect since it is the result of an explosion. Secondly, the big bang, therefore, also supports the minor premise that the *universe began to exist* or *the universe is a thing that came into existence*. The second law of thermodynamics or entropy also confirmed this. Furthermore, we saw that the quantum objection is really a non-objection. So the major premise, *anything that begins to exist has a cause for its existence*, seems to be scientifically sound. Can we agree on that?

S: So far, it looks pretty good.

B: To elaborate a bit more on a*gent causation,* try to imagine the universe coming into being.

S: Okay.

B: As it comes into existence, it would have done so at a *specific moment,* correct?

S: I suppose so.

B: If the universe, then, came into *being,* it could have done so prior to the moment you just conceived that it did, right?

S: Yes, and even after, for that matter.

B: I was just going to say that. Does it, then, not seem to follow that *whoever* or *whatever* brought the universe into existence must possess volition of *some* sort since the Cause could have done so at other moments?[23]

S: Yes, I guess so.

---

[23] If time began at "x", and at time "x" the universe came into being, then it seems that it could have come into being prior to time "x" and even after. Whoever caused the universe, it seems, could have caused it to come into being at other moments—this choosing of moments (logical sequence, not chronological) suggest that the cause possess volition of some sort. And if the cause possess volition, then the cause is personal.

B: That is one reason why some theists argue that the Cause [God] must be a personal agent.

S: I see. Boy, that was some mind-stretching stuff.

B: I know. Don't you love it? The philosophical proof is also quite intriguing.

S: As you know, even though I'm not a philosopher, I greatly enjoy philosophical reasoning. Let's hear it!

B: All right, then. Earlier you brought up the idea that perhaps the phenomenon of the universe expanding has been going on for infinity. And I said that if this was so, since the universe is destined to decay in a heat death, it should have burnt out an infinity ago.

S: Right.

B: Are you sure you are following me?

S: Yes, if the universe is infinite, but has been moving towards heat death for all infinity, it should have come to an end an infinity ago.

B: Exactly. And if it did, the universe would not have been here as it is now, it would have burnt up. So this notion is incoherent.

S: I concede the point.

B: But you know, some have argued that there may be an infinite number of causes and effects going back in time.

S: That could be a possibility, could it not?

B: I don't think so. For if this was possible, the series of events in the past would be endless or infinite.

S: Why could this not be?

B: Regarding this notion, philosopher William Lane Craig points out, "... the series of past events comes to an end in the present—but the infinite cannot come to an end." Second, "if the number of past events were infinite, that would lead to infinities of different sizes,"[24] which would be absurd.

S: Can we test one of those notions in a syllogism.

---

[24]Craig, William L. *Reasonable Faith* (Wheaton, IL: Crossway Books, 1994), pg. 80.

B: This is precisely what he does. He reasons that it is impossible for an actual infinite number of things to exist. Here is the argument in standard form,[25]

> (1) An actually infinite number of things cannot exist.
>
> (2) A beginningless series of events in time entails an actually infinite number of things.
>
> (3) Therefore, a beginningless series of events in time cannot exist.[26]

S: That follows, but it seems complex. Could you please clarify?

B: Certainly. It is actually not that difficult. As you can recall, there are two types of infinity. First, you have what is called a *potential infinite*. Counting would be potentially infinite since it had a beginning with the number one.

S: Right, I recall from a class on Set Theory.

B: So, counting would be one example of a potentially infinite since one can always add another finite number after another. And since it is, by illustration, moving towards infinity, it

---

[25] A *standard form argument* consists of two premises followed by a conclusion.

[26] Craig, Reasonable Faith., pg. 94

is potentially infinite but not actually infinite since counting will never reach infinity and infinity is endless in that regard.

S: What about an actual infinite?

B: An actual infinite would be something that actually is infinite. Suppose your coffee mug is of an infinite size. If it was, could it get any bigger?

S: Certainly not.

B: Why not?

S: Because it already is infinite and can thus not get any bigger.

B: Right. At a debate in Chicago, Dr. Craig raised a good question, he asked, "What is infinity minus infinity?"[27]   But here one gets self-contradictory answers. David Hilbert, the German mathematician argued,

> The infinite is nowhere to be found in reality. It neither exists in nature, nor provides a legitimate basis for rational thought. The

---

[27]The video: *Atheism Versus Christianity.* Recorded at Willow Creek Community Church, IL: Zondervan Publishing House, 1994.

role for the infinite to play is solely that of an idea.[28]

S: I love it.

B: I do too. Dr. Craig further elaborates, "but that entails that since past events are not just ideas but are real, the number of past events must be finite. Therefore, the series of past events can't just go back and back forever, rather the universe must have begun to exist."[29]

S: That really clarifies it.

B: Good. While there are other examples of the impossibility of an actual infinite in this sense, I think Hilbert's Hotel, as an illustration, will really put the thing to rest, or at least clarify. It goes something like this...

S: Hilbert's Hotel, what's that all about?

B: I was just going to tell you. That coffee is really working, isn't it? [Smile]

S: Make your point!

---

[28]*Ibid.*
[29]*Ibid.*

B: Well, Hilbert's Hotel consists of an infinite number of rooms. Imagine, for a moment, that all of the rooms are full, yet you are in need of a room.

S: Okay, I am in need of a room.

B: As you approach the entrance to the hotel, there is a sign on the door that reads "NO VACANCY—GUESTS WELCOME"[30]

S: How could this be?

B: That's what some mathematicians say.

S: Please render that as intelligible.

B: All right. In a nutshell, as I said, the rooms are all occupied, but if you requested a room, according to an actual infinite, Hilbert and Craig seem to maintain that it is possible to shuffle the guest in room #1 into #2, and the guest in #2 into #3 and so on for all infinity, thus making room for you in room number one, yet mathematicians argue you did not join #1. This is because you cannot add or take away from an actual infinite.

---

[30]Craig, *Reasonable Faith.*, pg. 96

S: That sounds so strange.

B: [Laughter] I know. And the point is that the whole notion of an actual infinite number of things is so absurd that to even think about it is sickening.

S: No kidding.

B: Another illustration may clarify a little better. Suppose you and I were on our way by flight to Gothenburg. For our purposes, then, say there are an actually infinite number of miles to get to Gothenburg.

S: All right.

B: But after we've been traveling for a quadrillion hours through storms, rain and turbulent conditions, I ask you "how far have we traveled?" according to an actual infinite you would have to say, "We have not even begun the journey" which of course seems so absurd, right?

S: To say the least.

B: Thus, you see, of course, infinitely speaking in this sense, we could not even begin our journey because there is no beginning nor end to an actual infinite, hence no presentness either. The infinite cannot cross the finite realm, so to speak. Although, it seems that an infinite being (God) could enter the finite realm since He is in another dimension and is a spiritual being. This, we would consider miraculous, of course.

S: I see.

B: As I have lectured on this to believers, another illustration I have found helpful to use is God's eternality in comparison to man's eternality. God is actually eternal while man is potentially eternal. In other words, God has existed for all eternity, but man will exist for all eternity. God had no beginning point, but since man had a beginning but will live for eternity, man is potentially eternal (or potentially infinite).

S: I get the picture.

B: Now, in like manner to our hotel illustration and God, to hold that there is an infinite number of causes and effects behind the universe is just as absurd.

S: Is this the type of stuff you have been studying while being gone?

B: To a degree, but let's stay on track. Do you now see that to argue that the series of events in the past are infinite cannot be and is thus not helping us in finding the answer?

S: We are certainly making progress, but I am still not convinced. If we grant that the universe had a beginning or is an effect, and that every effect has a cause, what then caused God?

B: I used to ask myself the same thing while pondering my salvific experience.

S: So what did you come up with? What caused God?

B: The answer is so simple that I am ashamed to say that I did not figure it out right away. But as I re-read one of my books on logic, I came across the section on Category Errors.

S: Right. I remember, "blue weighs more while sleeping slower than the drumming flute thinks about Wednesday smiling outside under the month of June during the winter holidays parallel with Manhattan in Malmo of airportness and nowness smells."

B: Boy, is that absurd or what? It almost sounds like an eastern slogan or proverb.

S: So what do category errors have to do with God and my question?

B: Well, since a category error entails asking something of something to which it does not apply, your question qualifies as a category mistake[31].

S: That's almost insulting. This better be good.

B: You asked what caused God, but I never claimed that He was an effect, thus He needs no cause.

S: That's trickery.

B: Oh, not at all. You see, you are misreading the main argument. Remember,

> Anything that begins to exist has a cause for its existence

> The universe is a thing that came into existence

> Therefore the universe has a cause for its existence

---

[31] One does not ask: "how much does the color green weigh?" Nor do we associate "speed" with "numbers" and thus, we do not claim that the principle of causality applies to God but only to things "that come into being"—that were caused. God is uncaused—eternal.

S: I know the argument pretty well by now.

B: Okay then, does the argument anywhere say that everything has a cause?

S: Mmmm... No.

B: It says anything that begins to exist has a cause, right?

S: And since you never claimed that God came into being, He needs no cause, and is therefore not an effect?

B: You got it. Like Moreland points out, "He [God] is a necessary Being and such a being does not need a cause."[32]

S: But if this is true of God, why can it not be true of the universe?

B: Because as we said, the universe began to exist, and an infinite number of things in the past cannot and does not exist.

S: Right.

---

[32]Moreland, *Scaling.* p.38

B: Thus, we see that rather than maintaining that the universe is infinite (infinite series of events in the past) it is much more plausible to believe in a first cause, himself being uncaused, as Aquinas said.

S: Why couldn't the universe have created itself?

B: Because it would have had to exist before it actually created itself, and is thus back to being infinite or eternal which is absurd.

S: Granted. I'll buy it. But what about the Oscillating Theory?

B: What about it?

S: I mean, not to discount all you have previously said, but is it not possible, according to this theory, that the universe indeed did not have a beginning?

B: The model of oscillation asserts that the universe expands endlessly and then contacts.

S: Right, as in a series of big bangs.

B: But this idea of the universe expanding and contracting infinitely is problematic. You see, there are no known laws or physical mechanism that could ever pull back or make the universe go into a state of re-collapses. Since the mass of the universe is expanding at such rapid pace and force, for it to ever pull back, gravitational laws unknown to us would have to exist. But this is unaffirmable and hence unscientific since science is based on observation or empirical evidence.

S: I see. What about the steady state model proposed by Herman Bondi, Thomas Gold and Fred Hoyle in 1948?

B: They were arguing from the idea of "continual creation." Astronomer Hugh Ross points out,

> In their models, the universe, though expanding indefinitely, takes on an unchanging and eternal quality since the voids that result from expansion are filled by the continual, spontaneous creation of new matter. Their proposal made the creation of matter no longer a miracle from the past, but an ongoing law of nature that can be tested by observations.[33]

---

[33] Moreland, J.P. Ed. *The Creation Hypothesis. Scientific Evidence for an Intelligent Designer.* (Downers Grove, IL: Intervarsity Press, 1994), pg. 146.

Ross points out several problems with this view. He points out that

(1) Due to the lack of very old galaxies near our galaxy; an infinite view of the cosmos is refuted. Moreover, since there is a "lack of very young galaxies near our galaxy", continual creation is negated.

(2) The "paucity of galaxies and quasars (distant celestial objects that radiate far more light than typical galaxies) beyondary a certain boundary implies that we are not living in an infinite steady state universe."

(3) The lack of a "physical mechanism (such as the primeval explosion)" able to cause the universe to expand, shows [or suggests] this model to be faulty.

(4) The background radiation (since the primordial "fireball" is cooling off) of the universe is evidence against the steady state theory.

(5) Due to the lack of entropy ("the measure of energy in a system that is

unavailable to perform work"), a
steady state universe is nonsensical.[34]

S: If that is so, then I admit, the steady state model
       is completely evacuated.

B: Dr. Ross further points out that this model of
       the universe is unable to explain the abundance
       of "deterium, light helium and lithium" but
       can be perfectly explained from a "big bang
       beginning." Finally, since we are observing the
       light of past galaxies and quasars, the steady
       state model is implausible.[35]

S: Not too strong, huh?

B: No. In addition, this theory totally presupposes
       that matter is eternal.

S: Fair enough. I'll concede your points.

B: Oh, you surrender, as in old times?

S: Hey, I got you to surrender just as many times.
       What else do you have in your theistic arsenal?

---

[34] *Ibid.*, pg. 148.
[35] *Ibid.*

B: I have a number of arguments in my bag. Are you willing to proceed, because I could go on all night?

S: Since this place is closing, let's go to my house and philosophize as we did in the past. I got this new set of patio furniture with insect lights and all, so mosquitoes won't bite us.

B: Sounds comfortable. Anything is better than that old green wooden bench of yours. I just look at it and it growls.

Good philosophy must exist, if for no other reason,

because bad philosophy needs to be answered

C.S. Lewis

Chapter Two

S: So, perhaps then, you could clarify some of my problems regarding God's existence, like rampant evil in the world. How God is all good, but yet He hates evil and is powerful enough to abolish it but won't.

B: You know, that has been called "the rock of atheism," and I do not take that issue lightly, I myself lost a son, and I could never quite figure out why God would let this happen. Like philosopher Thomas Morris says, "When crises arise, we philosophize."[36]

S: I did not know you had a son.

B: Well, I did not get to tell you because we have not talked for so long. But I did lose a son, and the truth is that I still wonder why it had to happen. I think all people do the same in a sense in that we wish it could be otherwise and are left with the question, "why God?" But it is

---

[36]Morris, Thomas V. *Making Sense of it All* (Grand Rapids, MI: William B. Eerdmans Co, 1992), pg. 34

something we all will have to learn how to cope with. Anyway, that is a question that deserves to be answered, but I cannot guarantee that we can solve it. I will show you how I personally deal with some of the problem(s) of evil, but let us first go through some of the other arguments for the existence of God.

S: I have to admit that I am a bit rusty on the theistic arguments. And I have a confession to make; I never really paid that much attention to them anyway.

B: That's too bad. But let me tell you one thing, it is always a good thing to get both sides on the issue.

S: What do you mean?

B: I mean, I have had atheist professors and theistic professors both give their two cents, and feel that a lot of good things that could have been said were not said at certain times.

S: The same, though, would be true of theists trying to give atheism a fair rendering. Too often, the straw man[37] is brought in.

---

[37]A *strawman* is where an issue or position is misrepresented

B: That is true to a certain degree. I mean, there are people in both camps not being fair to the other side, but I think this is either because of ignorance or bias.

S: Or a combination of both.

B: I must say, that you and I have always been able to talk about everything. This is very rare in this world; I really treasure our friendship.

S: Hey, I've missed you too. It's good that you're back.

B: I recently read an eye-opening book by philosopher Thomas V. Morris, the philosopher I just mentioned.

S: I have heard of him before. Didn't he write a book on God and the Philosophers or something?

B: Yes, he did, but the one I am talking about is Making Sense of it All, and the title really says everything. But in the beginning part of the book he says something very relevant to our discussion and the pursuit of truth, he writes,

>   When you stop to think about it, life can be very confusing. Imagine yourself a

victim of amnesia suddenly awakening from a deep sleep in the midst of some vast forest. Looking around, it seems that you are equipped for a journey of some kind, but you realize to your utter astonishment that you have no idea where you came from, how you got here, where in the world you are, or where you are going. You have no map or compass. And your surroundings seem, in various ways, very strange, even dangerous. If someone else were to appear on the scene who seemed to understand your situation and to have answers for all your questions, you'd listen. At least, if I were in such a position, I certainly would. And if this person described the location of our immediate environs in a way that made sense of that I could see and hear around me, I'd listen all the more intently to what he had to say about my origins, mission, and destination...[38]

Is this not a true picture of all of us?

S: It certainly depicts the human dilemma.

B: Is it not interesting that so many people do not even care one whit about these ultimate questions? I mean, they won't even hear any of

---

[38]Morris, *Making Sense.*, pg. 1

it. There is no desire whatsoever. It is almost like they don't care about the truth of anything.

S: Well, they're not lovers of wisdom. I can recall Blaise Pascal saying,

> Those who do not love truth excuse themselves on the grounds that it is disputed and that many people deny it.[39]

The issue is, as you said, they don't care, they are not lovers of truth, which is sort of stupid. I recently saw the movie First Knight, where Sean Connery makes an interesting remark to Richard Gere, "A man who fears nothing, loves nothing. If you love nothing, what joy is there in your life?"

B: That's good. I think Pascal's wager argument equally applies where he said that by believing in God we have all to gain and nothing to lose. It seems that if one truly loves oneself, then one will look into ultimate issues in the pursuit of truth in order to have true joy in life. To not fear the consequences seems rather foolish.

S: What is so interesting is the way so many reason. Like Pascal said, they discount truth because it is disputed and denied. But it

---

[39]*Ibid.* pg. 16

certainly does not follow that simply because something is disputed, truth can't be found, or that nobody is right.

B: I agree, it does not follow logically from disagreement that no one is correct. That would be like saying since astronomers disagree on the size of the universe, it has no size.

S: Exactly. In addition, many people make fun of those who claim to know something, but denial or even ridicule is not an argument either.

B: I know. That's when you want to ask "are you right in your denial of my claim?" It's self-refuting at best.

S: [Laughter]

B: Concerning man and issues of such vital importance, Pascal is quite insightful. He called it diversion and says,

> The only good thing for men therefore is to be diverted from thinking of what they are, either by some occupation which takes their minds off it, or by some novel and agreeable passion which keeps them busy, like gambling,

hunting, some absorbing show, in short by what is called diversion... We run heedlessly into the abyss after putting something in front of us to stop us from seeing it.[40]

S: It certainly is foolish, isn't it?

B: Yes it is. It reminds me of the Christian thinker, Ravi Zacharias, whom when he was a teenager, growing up in India, heard a strange chant which went something like this,

From the canyons of the mind, we wander on and stumble blind, wade through the often tangled maze of starless nights and sunless days, hoping for some kind of clue—a road to lead us to truth. But who will answer?...[41]

S: That sure seems lonely. What despair? I wonder if that isn't true of us all to a certain degree. Who is to blame here? God for hiding, or man for being ignorant?

B: Well, Dr. Craig in a debate commented on Pascal's view regarding the hiddeness of God, he said, God has given sufficient evidence of

---

[40]*Ibid.* pp. 33, 34

[41]Zacharias, Ravi. *Can Man Live Without God* (Dallas, TX: Word Publishing, 1994), pg. 3

His existence to every one with an open heart and mind, but this evidence is also sufficiently vague in order not to compel those people whose hearts and minds are shut.[42]

S: As in natural theology[43]?

B: I think so. But Jesus, I think, hit the nail right on the head when he said,

> "man loved darkness rather than the light." I believe that there is something rotten in man as it relates to his condition. After all, one does not have to teach a child to lie or rebel, it seems to come naturally. In like manner, when it comes to ultimate issues, man runs away from the truth, especially if it requires a change of living, even if it seems right, noble and true to do so.

S: Was it not Steven Turner, who wrote the cynical poem that read,

---

[42]William Lane Craig versus John Dominic Crossan, *Will The Real Jesus Please Stand Up! The Debate.* (Elgin, IL: Turner-Welninski Publishing, 1995), pg. 69.

[43] Natural theology is not the same as natural revelation (or general revelation). First, natural revelation is the disclosure about God based on the created order—this revelation is objective (independent of human reasoning). Second, natural theology is human knowledge about God derived from creation (natural revelation) and this type of theology is subjective since it involves human subjective reasoning.

> We believe that man is essentially good.
> It is only his behavior that lets him
> down. This is the fault of society.
> Society is the fault of conditions.
> Conditions are the fault of society.[44]

B: [Laughter] That's funny. Talk about circular reasoning. But is it not interesting that more people, except for people like you, don't pursue the questions? What apathy. This is true outside of the church as well as inside of church structures.

S: But what would you say to the person who said there is no truth? Like truth of any kind cannot be found, especially concerning God?

B: I would ask him if that statement were true.

S: So, there is at least one truth, the truth that there is not truth then?

B: Furthermore, any statement about God is a theological statement. One could thus ask: " is that very comment (there is no truth as it relates to God), in respect to theological truth, correct or true?"

---

[44]Zacharias. *Can Man Live.*, pg.43

S: I see what you're saying, or better, I hear what you are saying.

B: That's almost funny. I guess I forgot to laugh. Look, the relativist[45] can't win; no matter which way he goes. If he says, "there is no truth," then that would be false and he has said nothing of any substance much. On the other hand, if he says that THAT is true, then there is such a thing as truth, so he can't win. The whole thought process is self-refuting.[46]

S: It's like Jean Paul Sartre believing that there is no meaning, though, he meaningfully believed that.

B: Right. The statement that there is no meaning would have to be a meaningless statement, hence nothing has been said. I would have asked Sartre if he believed that.

---

[45] Here I am referring to the *epistemological relativist* who claims that "one cannot know anything for sure" or "there is no such thing as truth." First, does the person espousing knowledge (epistemology) relativism "know that"? Moreover, is the statement "there is no such thing as truth" indeed true? If not, then what he says is clearly false. If true, then there *is* such a thing as truth.

[46] A *self-refuting argument* is a statement that cannot fulfill its own standard. For example, "I can't say seven words in English," but I just did.

S: Well, let us flesh out some of the other arguments for God's existence. What about the Ontological argument?

B: I don't think the ontological argument is the strongest one. I would favor the cosmological, teleological, and moral arguments.

S: I can recall several different versions of the cosmological argument, but need a refresher.

B: I would be glad to talk about them as well. I think Thomas Aquinas' Five Ways are a good continuation. Shall we pursue them?

S: Let's do it. This is getting exiting. By the way, I have to tell you something. You are the first Christian that I know who is able to articulate his faith in a sensible fashion, and in doing so, it seems to actually stand in the market place of ideas.

B: The Christian Scriptures require of the believer to give a reasonable answer, an apologetic, a well thought out answer or defense for the hope that is within him; and this is presented in a gentle and respectful spirit.[47]

---

[47] 1 Peter 3:15; also see Philippians 1:16

S: I see. But don't many Christians object to rigorous thinking in relationship to theology and philosophical inquiry?

B: Sure, some do. However, I think this is because they have not critically thought through what they were saying. In other words, in their opposition to philosophical inquiry (which is necessary for theological inquiry), they themselves use the laws of logic. So, it is sort of a self-defeating point of view. They use logic in the process of trying to refute it.

S: I agree. It is sort of a fideistic position, isn't it? This attitude of "Take it all by faith and all will be fine." Moreover, how much faith is required, and how can one pick which faith to or system of though to follow without using reason in the process?

B: Good point. What's interesting with that line of reasoning is that the fideist maintains that one ought or should affirm one's way of thinking. In making his case, he will often use rational argument to prove his point.

S: And this entails the use of logic, of course.

B: Exactly. The use of logic and argument is inescapable. Those who oppose it actually end up affirming it in the process.

S: Sure is sloppy thinking.

B: I would say so. In addition, some of the heavyweight thinkers throughout the history of Christianity have greatly involved themselves in philosophical investigation in testing ideas and so forth.

S: That's true. You have St. Augustine, St. Anselm and Thomas Aquinas among others affirming your worldview.

B: Right. And nowadays, there is Plantinga, Moreland, W.L. Craig, J.M. Reynolds, Geisler, Thomas Morris, and many others.

S: That does lend some credibility towards theism, because after all, they are some of the most respected contemporary philosophers.

B: In particular as it relates to religion. And even if the believer does not want to get into some of these ideas, at least he should not criticize those who feel it is important. It's almost as if some believers are born attorneys, in the sense that they are concerned with evidence and would like to have it at their disposal when necessary. But most importantly they are grounded in why they believe what they believe, theologically and philosophically.

S: I see what you are getting at.

B: Furthermore, there is a big difference between indulging oneself in the writings of Socrates, Plato and Aristotle (though, I am of the view that much wisdom can be obtained here—for example about nature, deduction and morality), than to use the methodology of the philosophers. These methodologies, I believe, are based on logic, which is a transferable attribute from God.

S: Please explain. I am not sure about that one.

B: Well, if logic were not an attribute from God, then it would have to have been produced by evolution. But this seems unlikely because evolution does not think. To say that evolution does think, seems to imply theistic notions like that there is a "thinker" (God) behind it all. Indicating there is purpose, meaning (or just that there is meaning in thinking correctly) and a plan in creation. The very ideas that the evolutionist does not believe. So, his own philosophy does not stand up to even basic science.

S: Go on.

B: Besides, a further principle of causality says that the effect is never greater than the cause, but only less or at best equal. So, if the Darwinian says that he possesses cognitive faculties like perception and memory (and even) logic, but yet is the result of the random shuffling of molecules by means of evolution with no mind or designer behind it, the evolutionist is claiming to be greater than his cause which is absurd.

S: That is a pretty good argument, perhaps even more convincing than kalam.

B: Moreover, he cannot fully rely on his own thinking either.

S: Why is that?

B: Because, if the atheist or evolutionist is to remain consistent, he has to admit that his very own thinking is the byproduct of the random shuffling of molecules as well. Thus, not only he did not even choose to be an atheist, but also he does neither possess volition, because his thoughts are just the way they are because of chance. In other words, give him five minutes, and he may become a theist—if he of his environment takes that evolutionary turn. This is the picture we get if we grant evolution.

S: That's almost devastating.

B: [Laughter] I know. You see, the atheist has to borrow the theistic worldview before he begins to reason or even tries to rebut the theist.

S: Because order cannot come from disorder, and if logic is from God, then we can rely on it.

B: Exactly. But the skeptic would say if one has been deceived by his own senses, he should not ever fully trust them again.

S: Oh, you mean like looking down a railroad track and believing that the two rails are becoming one when in fact they are separate?

B: Precisely. That's an optical illusion. Or like putting an oar or a wooden stick in the water, and once it's below the surface it appears to be bent, but is actually straight.

S: Well, the skeptic seems to have a pretty good case, don't you think?

B: He's got a point, but further investigation or further knowledge seems to solve these optical illusions.

S: Do you mean investigation by going down the track to discover whether they are still separate?

B: Yes, or jumping into the water to find out if the wooden stick is really bent. It appears as though the stick is bent and the two rails intersect. But when this is the case, further investigation will solve the skeptic's argument.

S: In other words, by going up the railroad track one will discover that the tracks are really separate. That makes sense. Fair enough!

B: Have you noticed that while the skeptic holds that one should suspend judgment on all things, he has not suspended judgment on his own skepticism?

S: It's clearly self-defeating. Yes, he is not skeptical of his own skepticism.

B: According to philosopher Norman Geisler, what it boils down to is,

> ...the claim of the skeptic and agnostic that "truth is unknowable" is either:
>
> (1) a universal truth claim,
>
> (2) a particular truth claim, or

(3) neither a universal nor particular truth claim.

If it is a universal truth claim, then it undercuts itself, for it is claiming that no statements (including its own) can be made. If it is offered only as a particular truth claim, namely, that some (many, most, etc.) truths cannot be known, then it is self-consistent. However, in this case it does not eliminate the possibility that one can know or establish the truth of some other world view... If the skeptic claims he is making no truth claim at all with his recommendation to suspend judgment about all truth claims, then he must explain how a statement about whether truth is knowable can avoid being a truth statement.[48]

S: Is it that most people have not thought this through or they just don't care about believing the absurd?

B: This type of radical skepticism is clearly an indefensible system of thought. Geisler further reasons, "The very claim that the premise of skepticism ("all truth is unknowable") is not a truth claim would automatically disqualify it

---

[48]Geisler, Norman L. *Christian Apologetics* (Grand Rapid, MI: Baker Book House, 1976), pg. 134.

philosophically, for philosophy is concerned with truth."[49]

S: But what about the one who claims that we are all fallible and sometimes reason erroneously?

B: That proves my point. You see, "error" actually disproves skepticism. Peter Kreeft and Ronald K. Tacelli points out, "Error does not prove skepticism, it refutes it." Josiah Royce's essay ("The Possibility of Error" in The Religious Aspect of Philosophy) proved that the possibility of error is necessarily grounded in, and logically presupposes, the knowability of objective truth."[50]

S: That's really good. These guys have really thought about this issue, have they not?

B: You bet they have. Can you recall Rene Descartes' famous dictum Cogito ergo sum?

S: Oh, yes, meaning I think therefore I am.

B: Right. He was told to question all that he believed.

---

[49]*Ibid.*
[50]Kreeft, Peter. and Tacelli, Ronald K. *Handbook of Christian Apologetics* (Downers Grove, IL: InterVarsity Press, 1994), pg.. 368.

S: I wonder if the skeptics questioned that?

B: [Laughter] No kidding. Anyway, I think his argument is relevant to our discussion. Remember he went into an oven to meditate.

S: Yes, but the oven was probably not on though, right?

B: If it were, he surely would not have been able to produce the argument.

S: [Laughter]

B: In any event, as you probably recall, he began to question everything, even his own existence. Like how could he possibly prove that he was "not a butterfly in the midst of a dream" and so on.

S: That is so weird.

B: I know, but what is so interesting here is as he said, "When the principle, upon which a truth is established collapses, so does the very truth itself."[51]

---

[51]Cooney, Neil. *Greek And Latin Wisdom.* 1991, pg.80

S: So in other words, rather than questioning all of his views, he questioned the foundation for all of his thinking.

B: Right, and as he did, he began to doubt everything. And while philosophizing he came to this conclusion, namely, that he did not doubt the fact that he was doubting.

S: You mean he was sure of the fact that he was in doubt.

B: Exactly. That was the one thing he knew for sure. Thus, he thought, there are some things that can be known for sure. And since doubting entails thinking and thinking entails existence, he said, I think therefore I am—Cogito ergo sum.

S: I love Cartesian thought. Talk about deep.

B: I know, but it's a good point. What is so amusing with some people is that they say, "you can't know anything for sure." When the obvious response is "Do you know that for sure?"

S: [Laughter] But what about the person who says, "You can only know truth by means of scientific methodology"?

B: I would ask the person who made such a claim "What scientific methodology, then, is the grounds for that particular truth?" It is not "self-referentially coherent."

S: I see, but I have often heard nontheists claim that the burden of proof is always on the one making the claim.

B: If that is the case, then the skeptic better defend his skepticism, because now the burden is on him.

S: All right, then, but you have to admit that, a skeptic who claims, "Certainty comes only by adding a reason, a proof, to an idea. But the very proof depends on its premises being true. These, in turn, are certain only if proved by other premises, et cetera ad infinitum[52]. Thus nothing can be absolutely certain"[53] does have a case for his skepticism.

B: I don't think so, Kreeft and Tacelli points out,

> Aristotle answered the argument that all arguments must have an infinite regress of premises long ago. He said that the chain of premises does not stretch back infinitely because it ends at "first

---

[52] ...and so on, and so on, and so on...

[53] Kreeft and Tacelli, *Handbook.*, pg. 369.

principle," or "self-evident truths" which need not be proved by prior premises because they prove themselves... For the predicate arises necessarily from reflection on the meaning of the subject, as in, "A whole is greater than any of its parts".[54]

S: That makes sense, I think! But how does one know or come to know things?

B: First, there is, the correspondence theory of truth which is the idea that a given theory or proposition has to correspond to reality. And then, one can apply what is referred to as the coherence theory of truth in which the various propositions making up a theory cohere with each other. That is, the propositions have to be consistent with one another. These are two tests one may use; though there are some problems with these.[55]

S: I see. But they are helpful to a degree, though?

---

[54]*Ibid.*

[55] Regarding the *correspondence theory of truth* some have argued "How can I know that my idea correspond to its object if in fact it does?" Milton also points out that it has been argued that this view assumes a metaphysical unity, which may not be real. That is, it may not exist. As Russell points out, *coherence* may be a *test* or even *necessary condition* of truth but it is not what is *meant* by truth. see: Hunnex, Milton D. *Chronological and Thematic Charts of Philosophies and Philosophers.* (Grand Rapids, MI: Academie Books, 1986), pg. 7.

B: Yes they are.

S: What do you call all of this stuff?

B: What it really boils down to is epistemology.[56] We all have an epistemology.

S: I see. You know, you're right. We all do hold some beliefs, but I guess all of us do not test these beliefs. Rather, we go about thinking we are correct when in fact we may not be. Boy, that could have devastating results.

B: Yes, that is why one needs to make sure that (1) one's theory fits various facts; (2) make sure it does not contradict itself; (3) it has explanatory power; (4) is more plausible than competitive tentative assumptions; (5) has a wide range of arguments in its favor; (6) is able to refute other theories on related matters;[57] and (7) is not too complex or too simple as a system as a theory or hypothesis (especially as it relates to ultimate questions). Now, in all fairness, if one has complete evidence, which is very unlikely by the way, then knowledge is certain. But if one's

---

[56] *Epistemology* is a branch of philosophy concerned with knowledge. It is the study of knowledge; theories of knowledge as in *how we arrive at truth, what can be known and by what means.* i.e. *how* do we know *what* we know?

[57] Ravi Zacharia's, *A Shattered Visage, the Real Face of Atheism.* (Grand Rapids, MI: Baker Books, 1990), pg. 189-192 (Appendix 2 "The Establishment of a World View).

evidence is incomplete, then one's knowledge is only probable. This is where one enters into degrees of plausibility (what is most seemingly true in light of all), etc. as noted earlier.

S: Boy, that's a handful.

B: I know, but once these are in place mentally and in theoretical practice, it becomes easy to filter entire ideologies, or just general conversations, to find out how well versed the person you're talking to really is on the subject at hand.

S: That is good to know.

B: As Socrates used to say, "The unexamined life is not worth living."

S: I am starting to agree with you more and more. Especially after seeing the list of things you just shared. But I have to ask you something else, there seems to be so many different definitions of truth, how does one know which one to pick?

B: Well, the number of definitions doesn't mean much, whether they be many or few. But you are correct. There are various alternative theories of truth.[58] And some of these, as you

---

[58] Kreeft, *Handbook*, pp. 364-365.

shall see, are deeply problematic. There is, for example, the truth of the pragmatist who argues that "truth is whatever works for you." Pragmatism is a relativistic notion of truth and is subjective at best. However, something can be true even if it does not work or is not practical for you.

S: Hmm?

B: As G.E. Moore showed in his essay "William James's Pragmatism", the whole notion of truth-theory is linguistically confused. As Kreeft and Tacelli points out,

> There is a perfectly good word in the language for "what works." That word is "efficient" or "effective" or "practical." If we reduce truth to "what works," we lose a different, distinctive, independent Meaning of truth as "saying what is."[59]

S: Absurd indeed. But what about empiricism?

B: The empiricists theory of truth is grounded in our senses (touch, smell, see, hear, and taste). "Truth", as some, if not most, scientists say, "can only be known by means of a scientific experiment" that is empirically verified.

---

[59] *Ibid.* pg. 365.

S: If that is so, then what "empirical scientific experiment" leads the scientist to that particular truth?

B: That was going to be my next point. It is clearly self-defeating. But we should note that all empiricists do not claim to be relativists, although, to be consistent, they should be. In addition, as I alluded to earlier, these empiricists who only believe that truth can be known from the senses, really do believe in something else that is not verified by the five senses.

S: What's that?

B: They trust logic. In other words, the laws of logic like the law of noncontradiction (A cannot = non-A; of two propositions that are mutually exclusive or contradictory, both cannot obviously be true) and the law of excluded middle (A or non-A; any statement is either true or false—there is no middle ground here) are nonphysical laws that are unverified according to scientific criterion. You see, for the scientists to even construct criteria to test these laws the scientist is really relying on these laws in the process or before he comes up with his theories. Moreover, logic is nonphysical or intangible and can thus not be put in a test tube.

S: That makes sense.

B: Right. Furthermore, it does not take a rocket scientist to figure out that there is a difference between "the true" and "the sensible."

S: As in drugs causing hallucinations, for example?

B: Yes. These images are not true images.

S: What about the truth-theory of rationalism?

B: It also is troublesome because it is too extreme. Truth is not only what can be proven by reason. If it was, how could one prove that only truth could be proven?

S: Right, right, right. Just like the scientists rely on the laws of logic while going about his business, right?

B: Yes. The laws of logic, for example, are nonphysical or intangible yet they are real and true but cannot be shown to be true.

S: And why is that?

B: Because in trying to prove it you are affirming it in the process of doing so and are hence begging the question.[60] In other words, it's a circular argument.

S: I see. But I guess we have to be fair. Now, what about those who say, "truth is what I feel"?

B: That is the truth of emotivism. This is a common slogan among some cults and religions. I've seriously heard people say "I got this warm fuzzy feeling one night, therefore I know astrology [or whatever] to be true." This is so silly. The "feelings of fuzziness and warmth" do not equal what is necessarily true, regardless of what religion or worldview one holds. Some religious people claim that "I know this and that to be true because I can feel a burning in the bosom."

S: That could be the result of too much pepper on his eggs that morning.

B: No kidding. I mean, I do appreciate their zeal and sincerity, but to argue "truth is merely that which I feel " confuses "knowing truth" and "mere feelings." This notion of truth, by the way, is something that I have experienced in many high school "question and answer" settings.

---

[60] i.e. you *assume* that which you are trying to *prove*.

B: In addition, something can be true without you feeling it. For example, the fact that my car keys are in my pocket can be true even though I do not emotionally experience that truth about my dearly beloved keys, right?

S: I agree. I am reminded that one-person alone can also know a truth without the majority knowing it. The same thing about your keys can be used here. You alone may know where the keys are located but no one else may have that knowledge.

B: Exactly. An entire civilization can be wrong in their treatment of fellow human beings in a harsh way or in a lack of believing in God. It may still be that God exists or that Christianity is true regardless of the consensus of "hoi polloi."[61]

S: I see.

B: There is also the coherence theory of truth which holds that when a set or number of ideas correspond, one has found truth, as opposed to truth can be arrived at as the correspondence between a given idea and that idea's own

---

[61] The masses (the simple, majority).

external object,[62] as maintained by dualists (whom I'd agree with on this point).

S: What's wrong, then, with the coherence theory?

B: It's simply incoherent. You see, it presupposes that it is true on behalf of the correspondence of the dualistic picture it disagrees with and is hence irrational.[63]

S: Right, that seems to be a contradiction.

B: Yes it seems that way.

S: We surely covered a lot of ground, did we not?

B: We sure did.

S: But that is good to know.

B: Not just good to know, but good to practice. As Aristotle says, "It is the function of the wise man to know order [logos—order]." To that we

---

[62] Kreeft, *Handbook*, p. 365.

[63] There are other tests for truth in addition to these. See Geisler, *Christian Apologetics*, pp.141-142. *Unaffirmability as a Test for Falsity*, and *Undeniability as a Test for Truth (and Existential Undeniability)*. See also *Combinationalism, which* carries some plausibility.

can add: "And to put to practice that order," which is really what one would do if one knew order.

S: You're right. If we all practiced this, there wouldn't be so much "junk" to plow through in our "modernistic mindset conversations" just to make a point or get through an argument. But, Norman Cousins points out that this, to be sure, is not the era of meditative men and women.

B: But let us move on to some of the other arguments for God's existence. Enough about this.

S: You're right. Enough about this, I want to hear Aquinas' arguments for God's existence.

B: Great. But could we make some tea, it is starting to get late and I could really use a cup?

S: Sure, is Lipton® okay?

B: That's fine. Boy, did we get on a tangent or what?

S: Yes, but I think it was relevant to our discussion. If not, it was at least interesting.

B: Are you sure you want to stay up. It is getting awfully late?

S: Why, are you tired?

B: No, not really.

S: Let's talk some more, then.

B: You are a true inquirer my friend.

The greatest question of our time is not communism

versus

individualism;

not Europe versus America;

not even the

East versus the West.

It is whether man can

live without God

Will Durant

The Smile of the Dawn

Chapter Three

B: Now, Thomas Aquinas' first proof for the existence of God was based on motion. He argued that in the world that things are in motion. It is clear (in sensu) that things in motion are moved by something else since a thing cannot bestow motion upon itself. Whatever caused this thing to have motion must then also have been moved by something else. Since this cannot go on for infinity, according to Aquinas, there must have been a first mover, an "Unmoved Mover", who caused all of the other things to move or have motion. And this Unmoved Mover, Aquinas believed, was and still is God. Pretty clever isn't it?

S: I sort of recall the argument. But please clarify the part about things not being able to move themselves.

B: Okay, things that are not in motion, according to Aquinas, are potentially in motion. But once a thing that is at rest is moved, then it is actually in motion. It had to be actualized, so to say, by something other than itself. This was his distinction between potentiality and actuality.

S: This Unmoved Mover, then, would have to be a Being of pure actuality, granting that this something is someone, right?

B: Exactly. God, in that sense, is pure actuality because if He was in a state of potentiality, then He would be just as the other potential things in motion. This is absurd for the simple reason that no thing that is potentially in motion can actualize something else that is potentially in motion.

S: Sort of like dominos lined up but later falling one after another in that each domino is the cause of the next one falling and so on, right?

B: I don't think that's what Aquinas had in mind. He was advocating that the causes are simultaneously acting together much like the gears do in a watch.

S: Is God, then, a gear in the watch or a part of the watch?

B: No, God could be likened to the spring that causes all of the gears to have motion. But in addition, of course, God is the Watch-Maker, like William Paley said.

S: What is his third proof?

B: Here Aquinas argued from the necessity of an absolutely necessary Being from the existence of possible things or Beings. He points out that in the world we notice that there are Beings. Possible Beings whose existence is not necessary at all.

S: What in the world does that mean?

B: You mean possible Beings[64] versus a necessary Being?[65]

S: Yes.

B: What Aquinas is trying to say is that there are things or beings, possible beings or things, which do not have to exist. That is to say, their existence is not necessary because these beings are contingent or dependent on something else

---

[64] Possible beings are beings that could at one time or another not have existed, Human beings are possible beings—it could have been the case that humans never came into being.

[65] A necessary being is the opposite of a possible being. A necessary being cannot *not exist*. It must exist and cannot come to an end. A necessary being exists of necessity.

for their existence and could not have existed without the contingent Being present first.

S: As in teleology?

B: Yes. But the main point of this argument is that if all things were indeed possible, then all of these things could cease from having existence. But Aquinas maintained that these possible things are not self-existent and thus owe their existence to something else that cannot also be possible but must, therefore, be absolutely necessary. And we call this absolutely necessary being, Aquinas and the rest of us, God.

S: If that was the case, then God's nature would have to be one of necessity, right?

B: Exactly his point, God is a necessary being in that God cannot not exist. Alvin Plantinga[66] does a nice schematization of this argument:

> (a) There are at present contingent beings ("things that are possible to be and not to be")

---

[66] Plantinga, Alvin. *God and Other Minds. A Study of the Rational Justification of Belief in God.* (Ithaca and London: Cornell University Press, 1967), pg. 5-6.

(b) Whatever can fail to exist, at some time does not exist.

(c) Therefore if all beings are contingent, then at one time nothing existed—from (b).

(d) Whatever begins to exist is caused to begin to exist by something else already existing.

(e) Therefore, if at any time nothing existed, then at every subsequent time nothing would exist—(d).

(f) Hence if at one time nothing existed, then nothing exists now—(e).

(g) Hence if all beings are contingent, then nothing exists now—(c), (f).

(h) Therefore, not all beings are contingent—(a), (g).

(i) Hence there is at least one necessary being—(h).

(j) Every necessary being either has its necessity caused by another being or has its necessity in itself.

(k) It is impossible that there be an infinite series of necessary beings, each of which has its necessity caused by another.

(l) Therefore there is a necessary being having of itself its own necessity, and this all men speak of as God—(i), (j), and (k).[67]

S: That's a mind-blowing syllogism.

B: Indeed it is. You see some of the others he addresses in his writings. Now, did the syllogism help ("a" through "k")?

S: I think so. I may have to think about it some more. But this raises another question of mine. If God is all-powerful, is he then not able to eliminate His own existence, which you say is necessary?

---

[67] There has been criticisms raised regarding this argument. Commentators of Aquinas disagree on their interpretation. Plantings does a fair job in addressing the disagreements in his *God and Other Minds*.

B: No, because that is logically impossible. If a being is necessary by its very nature, then this being cannot also be non-necessary at the same and in the same way. This would be the law of noncontradiction at work.[68]

S: I guess, then, that the same would be true of God being able to create a square circle?

B: Right, this He cannot do, but this is not a limitation of His power. You see, when theists say that God is all powerful they are not saying that God can do all things that we as human beings command of Him to do.

S: Give me an example.

B: Let's see. Take the issue of God being able to sin. Some people argue "if God can do all things, can he then sin?" But this is silly because God, by definition, is perfect and a Being that is perfect cannot do that which is imperfect. That is, a being whose very nature is that of absolute holiness, perfection and righteousness cannot commit evil.

---

[68]*The Law of noncontradiction* (a law of logic) states that "A" cannot equal "Not-A" which is to say that a thing cannot be what it is not. For example, a thing cannot *exist* and *not* exist at the same time and in the same way. Take a candle, for instance, it cannot *be* lit and *not be* lit at the same time and in the same way. This law distinguishes all of human thinking. It is impossible to deny this law because in trying to do so, one will only affirm it in the process.

S: Then it is sort of lame to ask if a perfect being can do that which is imperfect.

B: Precisely my point. The same is true of the paradox of the stone. Here some argue, concerning the omnipotence[69] of God, that if God is all powerful could He create a rock that is so big that He Himself is unable to lift it.

S: I have heard Christians respond "Sure, God can do anything."

B: That's because they have not thought through critically what they are saying. God cannot do that which is contrary to His own nature which is to say that God, also then, cannot do that which is logically impossible.

S: That makes a lot of sense.

B: So, to finish our example of the paradox of the stone, if God is the most powerful being, then He, by definition, cannot create something more powerful than Himself.

S: So what's the point here for the person who raised the question in the first place?

---

[69]By omnipotence we mean *all powerful.*

B: Well, the person who argues this way thinks in his self-proclaimed brilliance, that he's got the theist in a corner without realizing his own folly.   You see, if the believer in God says, "sure, God can do that" then the nontheist says "Well, then God cannot do all things, and is thus not all powerful." And if the theist says, "No, God can't", then the atheist responds "I guess God is not all powerful." But he misses the point of logical impossibility.

S: I understand it much better now. But isn't this just a matter of semantics?

B: No, it is the nature of thought[70] all together. To argue the opposite only affirms my position in the process.

S: How in the world did we get into all of this?

B: You are the one who asked if God could eliminate His own existence.   That's how we

---

[70] As theists we believe that God wounded up the universe, and that this universe is subject to the laws of logic (*Law of Identity:* A=A, or "a thing is what it is;" *Law of noncontradiction:* A cannot = non-A, or "a thing cannot be what it is not (I can't walk on two feet while not walking on two feet at the *same time* and in the *same way*);" and the *Law of Excluded Middle:* A or non-A, or "any statement is either true or false (God exists—this statement is either true or false)." To argue against the laws of logic is impossible because one is using these laws in the process of making one's point—hence, self-refuting. These laws are inescapable, and these laws are trustworthy because they are grounded in the nature of God.

got into this. But since this is often a misunderstanding among theists and atheists alike, it was worth the discussion, don't you think?

S: I'd say so.

B: Let's go back to Aquinas. Remember he was arguing from the impossibility of infinite regression of causes to the establishment of a first cause. He does the same here. He argues that there has to be an absolutely necessary being who caused all of the other possible things or beings to exist.

S: So Aquinas' first three proofs, then, are based on cosmology in a sense, eh?

B: Right.

S: What was his next argument?

B: His fourth proof was based on the notion of perfection. Here he argued that there are degrees of perfection.

S: That's right, I remember, some things are more good, true and noble than other things.

B: Yes, and if one compares the things that are more good, true and noble with the things that are less good, true and noble, we find a gradation or degrees of perfection. Thus, Aquinas argued, there must be a most good, most true and a most noble. This Being must, therefore, be the Being of all beings, or the most being, so to say.

S: So, God would be the maximum genus of all things, then?

B: That's correct.

S: Did Thomas Aquinas think up all of these things by himself?

B: Actually, much of what he wrote has its roots in Aristotelian thought. He essentially "Christianized" the writings of Aristotle which is probably what I would have done if I got a hold of Aristotle's work in Aquinas' day. [Laughter]

S: But don't many theologians and Christians in general criticize him for that?

B: Oh, many do, and I disagree with them for the simple reason that Aristotle was left with the same general revelation as you and I are left with. And from this general revelation one can develop a natural theology.

S: What do you mean?

B: General revelation is the doctrine that God's existence is evident from creation. King David said, "The heavens declare the glory of God; And the firmament shows His handiwork."[71]

Paul (A.D. 57) also stated:

> For since the creation of the world His invisible attributes are clearly seen, being understood by the things that are made, even his eternal power and divine nature, so that they are without excuse.[72]

S: I see.

B: Can you recall the German philosopher Gottfried Wilhelm Leibniz?

S: No, but wasn't your father's name Wilhelm?

B: You remember. That's pretty good. After all, it's been so long. Anyway, one of the greatest

---

[71]Psalm 19:1 (NKJV)
[72]Romans 1:20

questions Gottfried Leibniz ever raised was "Why is there something instead of nothing at all?" John Calvin held that God's existence is known by all of man. As David Clark puts it, "God's truth about himself is scattered all over creation. This truth about God is, thus evident to all. We can all see it, Calvin maintained, both the learned man and the ignorant person."[73]

S: Do you believe that if one acknowledges God's existence from creation, one will go to heaven?

B: I don't believe this, although it doesn't really matter what *I* think. According to the Christian Scriptures, this knowledge of God is not salvific. It takes *special revelation* to inherit the kingdom of the living God.

S: What do you mean "special revelation"?

B: By special revelation I mean that God has revealed Himself to a certain group of people in history. He has revealed *why* one needs redemption and *how* this redemption can be obtained.

S: Why would God only reveal this information about himself to some people and not everyone?

[73]Clark, David L. *Dialogical Apologetics* (Grand Rapids, MI: Baker Books, 1993), pg. 10.

B: First of all, God is accessible to all of mankind. Secondly, if one responds to general revelation, then special revelation will be granted. Thus, I don't believe "Elvis Presely Theology." Meaning, that God is evasive and we can't know whether we ever really heard/saw Him. Unlike religious pluralism, where almost all will make it to heaven regardless of contradictory beliefs.

S: Elvis Presley theology, huh?

B: [Laughter] That's what I call it. Not that Elvis necessarily held that view, but it's almost as though God, according to pluralism, is playing games in that He won't reveal himself fully to mankind but only certain limited aspects of Himself, if even that.

S: At least it sounds politically correct.

B: It surely is, but theologically absurd, and rooted in nothing but mere subjective notions about ultimate reality. This is due to the lack of special revelation. But I would hold that if one responds to the knowledge of God in creation, then God in all fairness will grant special revelation. All one has to do is to draw near to God, and more light will be given.

S: Fair enough. What was Aquinas' fifth proof?

B: This one is based on the order of the cosmos. This is his teleological argument for the existence of God. Aquinas maintained that in nature, it is quite evident that things are moving toward some type of end or goal. Yet we also note that some of these things lack cognitive faculties or are consciousless, yet these mindless things are moving towards an end as though they had a purpose or goal. How is this so?

S: You mean like an acorn moving toward the goal of eventually becoming an oak tree?

B: Yes, and the interesting thing to notice here is that, this acorn, for example, seems to lack consciousness and yet it is progressing towards an end or goal. This goal is its purpose.

S: Right, the acorn's purpose is to become an oak tree.

B: And since this acorn is conscious*less*, there must be something conscious behind this whole operation of moving towards its goal. And, Aquinas concludes, this conscious or intelligent something behind this direction *is* God Himself.

S: Oh boy, this is very interesting. Should we have another cup of tea before we hit the sack?

B: No thank you, I won't sleep as good if I have another cup. Is it okay if I sleep on your couch?

S: Sure, that is expected. By the way, did you bring any clothes for tomorrow?

B: Yes, I have an extra set of clothes in my bag.

S: Good. What other arguments do you have for God's existence?

B: We ended on Aquinas' teleological argument, but there are others of the same nature produced by other thinkers.

S: Let's hear them.

B: All right, then. William Paley in his *Natural Theology*, says that if one were to cross a field [or walking on the moon] and stub one's toe against a stone. Most would not even question why or how the stone got there. But suppose one found a *watch*. Immediately one would question how the watch got there.

S: Well, perhaps the wind blew for a long time and eventually the rubbing of sand particles and other debris caused this watch to come into existence. You know, as in evolution.

B: I never expected you to say that.

S: Call me the Devil's advocate.

B: Since evolution is mindless, it cannot think, plan, or decide, it's just randomness or chance at work. Why in the world would anyone think that this watch, loaded with energy (potential energy), with fine tuned or adjusted elastic springs and gears and all, whose purpose it to give time, could be produced by consciousless evolution?

S: "You really got me now."

B: Believe it or not, some people would not find trouble in believing what you just said. Anyway, according to Paley, a watch must have a watchmaker, and what is designed must have a designer. The point here is that if it follows that behind the existence of this watch there is a watch-maker, then there must be a designer behind this universe as well, which by the way is far *more complex* than a watch with a few springs and gears.

S: I see the weight of the argument.

B: Once I heard an illustration of evolution. It went something like this; "a tornado blowing through a junkyard won't result in the assembly of a 747 Jumbo-Jet, or a SAAB plain engine with all of its sophisticated gismos."

S: [Laughter] No kidding. Just like the blowing up of a print shop won't result in an encyclopedia. But is this really a fair rendering of evolution?

B: Granted, I am not an evolutionary biologist, but as we said earlier, the effect is never greater than the cause (and information and design do *not* come from *non*mind). Thus, if mind or cognitive faculties were produced by evolution, which itself lacks a mind (if there was a mind behind evolution this would be the mindful being that theists call God), then the effect is now greater than the cause which is absurd. The notion that thinking can come from nonthinking is so improbable if not impossible. And if it were possible, there would still be no good reason to trust our own thinking or beliefs since they are only one of many potential results of a random, mindless cause.

S: That makes sense. But are you not presupposing certain *a priori* [74] truths?

B: Definitely. There are certain synthetic *a priori* truths that we all presuppose. For example,

[74] Prior to looking at the facts.

philosopher of science J.P. Moreland lists several of these in his book *Scaling the Secular City*. He writes,

➤ Something cannot come from nothing (out of nothing, nothing comes).
➤ There must be as much reality in a cause as in an effect.
➤ A cause must resemble its effect.
➤ Meaning or information must come from a mind.
➤ Parts do not cooperate toward ends unless they were put together by a planner for that end.[75]

S: That seems self-evident.

B: Yes, and to argue the opposite is counter-intuitive. Moreland, thus, further argues,…if one accepts as a synthetic a priori truth the statement "meaning of information must come from a mind," then if DNA contains information, it follows that this information has to come from a mind.[76]

S: But I really like the argument from the mind. That's very stimulating.

B: That is precisely what Alvin Plantinga argued when giving his lecture *An Evolutionary Argument Against Naturalism*.

---

[75] Moreland, J.P. *Scaling the Secular City*. Grand Rapids, MI: Baker Book House, 1987), p. 57.
[76] *Ibid.*

S: It almost seems as though a person's thought patterns are just randomly scattered around in the brain, so to say.

B: Yes, the neurons are just fired around in the human brain producing various thoughts, thus it seems as though one does not even have volition or free-will to choose one idea over another. In that case, the evolutionist never really chose to believe in evolution, but just believes it because the thoughts in his brain were randomly coalesced that way.

S: That sounds so absurd.

B: It is absurd. Just to add another thought. If our thoughts were just the product of neurons firing in the brain, then perhaps all atheists would become theists five minutes from now. Granting, of course, that thoughts were simply rearranged.

S: I get the picture, all right. It seems utterly silly. But how would you respond to the person who says, "if you put a billion monkeys by a billion typewriters with a billion gallons of ink, and then give it a billion years. Eventually, one of these monkeys will write Plato's *Republic* by chance?" This is often an argument in favor evolution.

B: I've heard a similar argument before. First, what strikes me is that the person who reasons that way *never* assumes that's how Plato's *Republic* came to be when he reads it. In other words, when one looks at *The Republic*, one does not conclude that it was written without intelligence. Perhaps it is *theoretically possible* (mathematically speaking), but who in his right state of mind would buy into such an incredibly improbable explanation for the cosmos? Talk about long leaps of faith!

S: It does seem a bit stretched.

B: It's more than "a bit stretched." You see, the atheist has no logical explanation for the universe. Perhaps the atheist needs a psychological explanation at this point.[77]

S: You're funny.

B: The atheist would probably not agree with you.

S: {Laugher] Probably not.

B: By the way, Plantinga also maintains that belief in God is *properly basic*.

---

[77] Kreeft, Peter. "The Rationality of Belief In God." Lecture. Forum, Texas A & M, TX.

S: Properly basic? What in the world does that mean?

B: Belief in God as properly basic essentially means that one is justified in believing in God *without* the proofs you and I have looked at.

S: What do you think about that?

B: I think Plantinga has a point. What about my mom, for example? She lives in a remote part of Europe and has never come across these arguments at all.   Is she not justified in believing in God without all of these proofs?

S: If, as you say, Calvin was right, then she is justified.

B: Right, if you recall our discussion on general revelation, the existence of God may be self-evident to her, —something she not only knows intuitively, but also from creation. In this sense, her belief in God is properly basic.   As Plantinga himself says, "When the Reformers claim that this belief is properly basic, they do not mean to say, of course, that there are no justifying circumstances for it, or that it is in that sense groundless or gratuitous."[78]

S: That's interesting. Now, how far did we go with the teleological arguments?

B: Well, an earlier version of the teleological argument can be found in Plato and Aristotle. Plato, for example, maintained that there was order in the motion of the stars, and concluded that there had to be a mind behind this ordered universe. Aristotle too, came to the conclusion that a divine and intelligent cause of the majestic breath-taking cosmos existed.

S: I think the teleological arguments are more convincing than the others are.

B: I personally favor the cosmological arguments which, by the way, remind me that we did not get into Leibniz version of the cosmological argument, nor did we talk about William Soreley's moral argument.

S: I got nothing to lose. My coffee is already cold. But before you share about Leibniz, what about scientific confirmations? Are there any scientific proofs or scientific support?

B: Sure there are. For example, astronomer Hugh Ross gives three main facts agreed upon by

Publishing, 1993), 95. See also "Is Belief in God Properly Basic?" in *NOUS* 15 (1981), pp. 41-51. Alvin Plantinga is the John O'Brien Professor of Philosophy at the University of Notre Dame.

most scientists, in particular, astronomers. First, *the universe is not infinitely old* as many maintain. An infinitely old universe, as we saw in the *kalam* cosmological argument, according to Ross, "has no foundation in reality."[79]

S: What are the other two facts?

B: Ross also points out that, "The universe can be traced back to a single, ultimate origin of matter, energy, time, and space (with the dimensions of length, width, and height)...The cause of the universe...who brought the universe into existence—existed and created from outside (independent) of the matter, energy, and space-time dimensions of the universe."[80]

S: That's pretty complex.

B: There is indeed an intelligent designer behind it all.

S: I think Maimonides had a point when he said study astronomy and physics to comprehend

---

[79] Ross, Hugh. *Creation and Time.* (Colorado Springs, CO: Navpress, 1994), pg.126
[80] *Ibid,.* pg. 127

the relation between the world and God's management of it.[81]

B: As Sir James Jeans said, "...the universe appears to have been designed by a pure mathematician..."[82]

S: That was Sir James Jeans, huh?

B: Sir Fred Hoyle also had something to say about the mastermind behind it all. He says, "...a super intellect has monkeyed with physics, as well as with chemistry and biology."[83]

S: What is the third fact?

B: The third fact goes well with Maimonides. According to Ross, astronomers reason,

> The universe, our galaxy, and our solar system exhibit more than *sixty characteristics that require exquisite fine-tuning* for their very existence, and also for the existence of life (any kind of life, not just life as we know it). They

---

[81] Maimondies. *The Guide for the Perplexed.*

[82] Jeans, Sir James. *The Mysterious universe,* Cambridge University Press, pg. 181.

[83] Hoyle, Sir Fred. *"The Universe, Past and Present Reflection,"* Annual Reviews of Astronomy and Astrophysics, 20:16 (1982).

> conclude that, "The eternity (Creator) who brought the universe into existence must be *personal, intelligent, powerful, and caring—personal, intelligent, and powerful, for only a super-intelligent, super-powerful Person* [a being with personhood][84] *could design and manufacture what we see, including life; caring, for only care could explain the enormous investment of creative effort, the attention to intricate detail, and the comprehensive provision for needs.*[85]

S: That's pretty convincing. Was it not Paul Davies who said, "I see powerful evidence that there is something going on behind it all? The impression of design is overwhelming"[86]?

B: It sure was. But, let's go back to the big bang model. Have you heard of the satellite known as COBE (meaning *Cosmic Background Explorer*)?

S: I've heard of it, it was a $200 million project, but I am not certain I know what it is fully about.

---

[84] Brackets are mine.

[85] Ross, *Creation.* pg.127

[86] Davies, Paul, *The Cosmic Blueprint* (New York: Simon and Schuster, 1988), pg. 203.

B: Well, as it relates to the question of whether the universe began to exist (and if it does, then it needs a cause as noted earlier), COBE seemingly confirms the theory—that the universe was birthed or began to exist.

S: How so? Could you please explain "Cosmic Background"?

B: Fred Heerin points out,

> "Cosmic" means it has the entire universe as its source. "Microwave radiation" is defined as radio waves with wavelengths shorter than one meter. And the word "background" simply tells us that it can be measured everywhere.[87]

> Now, COBE discovered that the universe must have been birthed or have come into being because of measurements of "fluctuations in the background radiation."[88]

S: Please, go on.

---

[87] Heerin, Fred. *Show Me God. What The Message of Space Is Telling Us About God.* (Wheeling, IL: Searchlight Publication, 1995), pp. 132.
[88] *Ibid.*, pg. 141.

B: Astrophysicist George Smooth at Lawrence Berkley Laboratory told Mr. Heerin in an interview,

> In order to make the universe as bid and beautiful as it is—we're talking fifteen billion[89] years and we're talking huge distances here—in order for it to be that big, you have to make it very perfectly. Otherwise, the imperfections would mount up and the universe would either collapse on itself or fly apart, and so it's actually a precise job. And I don't know if you have had discussions with people about how critical it is that the density of the universe come so close to the density that decides whether it's going to keep expanding forever or collapse back, but we know it's within one percent.[90]

There's so much to say here, but you get the idea.

S: Now we're talking! Now you have given me some scientific proof coming right from the mouths of the experts, and even a satellite, this is getting better, I must admit.

---

[89] There is a great deal of disagreement among some people regarding the age of the universe, but setting these disputes aside, the fascinating part is that the universe came into being pointing to a First Cause (God) outside of our space and time domain.

[90] Heerin, *Show Me God.* Pg. 142.

B: You like the science aspect too, huh?

S: I have never heard that science, philosophy and religion can go together. If it's not some radical extremist religious person being frightened of science or calling science evil like the weirdo's do in the movie *Contact*, it's a biased scientist totally discounting philosophy and religion. This is because of his own presuppositions. But you seem to have tied some of this stuff together. I like that.

B: I don't know if you have heard of Robert Jastrow?

S: Yes I have. He is a NASA scientist, isn't he?

B: Yes he is. He said with regards to his fellow astronomer friends,

> For the scientists who have lived by his faith in the power of reason, the story ends like a bad dream. He has scaled the mountains of ignorance; he is about to conquer the highest peak; as he pulls himself over the final rock, he is greeted by a band of theologians who have been sitting there for centuries.[91]

---

[91] Jastrow, Robert, *God and the Astronomers*, second ed. (New York & London: W.W. Morton & Company, 1992), pg. 292.

S: [Laughter] This is sure different from Carl Sagan who said, "The cosmos is all there is, or ever was, or will be..."[92]

B: No kidding it's different. When I first heard of Sagan making that statement I thought, "who is he to say that *the cosmos is all there is*? Was he there?" and "what does he know about the future concerning *what will be* anyway?"

S: I see the point. A strong claim for a mere man to make indeed!

B: But perhaps the most interesting statement made in all of this, concerning all of this proof, came from Jastrow when he said, "Most remarkable of all, astronomers have found proof that the universe sprang into existence abruptly, in a sudden moment of creation, as the Bible said it did."[93]

S: That is a heavy statement. I guess there is more to belief in God than just taking it by *faith*?

B: I like what J.P. Moreland says about faith. It is, "a power or skill to act in accordance with the nature of the kingdom of God, a trust in what

[92] Sagan, Carl. *Cosmos.* (Random House, New York, 1980), pg. 4.
[93] Jastrow, Robert. *Journey to the Stars,* (Bantam Books, 1989), pg. 43.

we *have reason to believe is true."* Thus, "...faith is *built* on *reason."*[94]

S: I have never heard of that definition.

B: Perhaps this is because you have only been around certain individuals who don't have a clue as to what rational theists believe.

S: Christian theism is actually more convincing than I thought it would be.

B: I know. Thus far, we've seen that not only is the Christian view of the universe *philosophically* plausible but *scientifically* persuasive. And, most importantly, biblical[95] as well. This ought to strike at the heart as a major step toward accepting Christian theism as *the* logically tenable worldview, at least with regard to the cosmos. This may be a good beginning, and then move on to salvific-claims and then look into the evidence for the reliability of the Judeo-Christian Scriptures.

---

[94] Moreland, J.P. *Love Your God With All Your Mind.* (Colorado Springs, CO: NAVPRESS, 1997), pg. 25

[95] Genesis 1:1 "In the beginning [*time*] God [*first cause, himself uncaused*] created [*ex nihilo-from nothing*] the heavens [*space*] and the earth [*matter*]." Also see: Gen. 1:3; Psalm 103:25, 26; 104:1-2; Isaiah 42:5; 45:12: Isaiah 51:6; Nehemiah 9:6; Matthew 24:35; 2 Timothy 1:9; Hebrews 4:3-4 for a few examples.

S: Perhaps, but what about evolution, though? Doesn't evolution disprove God's existence?

B: Not at all. Especially not in light of all we have seen thus far. But in any case, what about evolution? One could certainly argue that God used evolutionary means, although, I don't believe it. But, once again, this should not to be confused with *microevolution* (the change *within* a species) as opposed to *macroevolution* (the change from one species to *another species*). In addition, if evolution were true, it would be a miracle, and thus evidence for God's existence, because only God could bring about something so incredibly astronomically improbable.

S: I see. So what is this proof from the Judeo-Christian scriptures, then?

B: As it relates to the beginning of the universe, the Christian scriptures clearly states that it did come into being.[96] It is also clear that the cause

---

[96] Genesis 1:1 says, "In the beginning God *created* the heavens and the earth." The word created entails that the heavens and the earth, the universe, came into being. And the cause who created this event or effect is God. Thus the Bible confirms what philosophers call philosophical agent causation. It is also in agreement that time began (2 Timothy 1:9 "before time began").

of the universe is an eternal and personal agent.[97]

S: I see.

B: To a degree, perhaps.

S: How would you respond to those who argue against the Christian Scriptures claiming it's a "flat-earth" book?

B: That's community secular university "preaching." People who advocate that position *bow* to hearsay in order to have an argument, any argument for that matter, against Christianity. The oldest book of the Bible, according to most theologians, seems to be the Book of Job of which...

S: Wait a minute, you mean as the Book of Job in the movie *Mission Impossible* where Tom Cruise makes it possible to pull off the impossible?

B: Right. That was an intense movie, wasn't it? Anyway, Job said that the earth is a sphere

---

[97] It is evident that the cause possesses an intellect according to the Judeo-Christian Scriptures (see Genesis 18:19; Exodus 3:7. This cause also possesses volition (Genesis 3:15; Psalm 115:3).

hanging on nothing.[98] This seems to suggest that the earth is a sphere-planet resting in the universe.

S: Job said that? He certainly could not have used a telescope. That's very interesting. But what about the Bible referring to "the Four Corners of the earth" or Jesus being shown "all of the kingdoms of the world" while being tempted?

B: The Bible uses *metaphorical* [99] language just like we do today. For example, all of us, especially weather reporters, say things like "the sun will *rise* at 6:12 A.M." yet we know that the sun does not rise, but rather the earth goes around the sun.

S: That makes more sense. But what about other believing scientists, are there any well-known scientists who believe or believed?

B: Well, in addition to what we have seen, there are at least fifty believers, who by the way, have *led* the way of science, but this, of course, is something most people don't like to mention. This is obvious in most textbooks, whether it be high school or college books.

---

[98] "He spreads out the northern skies [...stretches out the north over empty space NKJV] over empty space; he suspends the earth over *nothing* (Job 26:7 NIV).

[99] A metaphor is a figure of speech.

S: Who are some of these scientists?

B: You shouldn't have asked, [Laughter] There is, Louis Agassiz (1807-1873)—the father of glacial science, William Foxwell Albright (1897-1971) —foremost archaeologist of the 20th century, Charles Babbage (1792- 1871)—who created the computer, Francis Bacon (1561-1626)—the forerunner of the scientific method, John Bartram (1699-1777)—first American botanist, Sir Charles Bell (1774-1842)—first to extensively map the brain and nervous system, Robert Boyle (1635-1703)—chief founder of modern chemistry, William Buckland (1784-1856)— foremost English geologist before Charles Lyell, George Cuvier (1769-1832)—founder of the studies of paleontology and comparative anatomy, John Dalton (1766-1844)—father of modern atomic theory and the list of believing scientists goes on and on.[100]

S: Fair enough! I am fairly impressed by these figures *and* previous evidences. But how old do you think the earth is, are you an *old earther* or a *young earther*?

B: That really is irrelevant. Believers have asked me the same question. You see, if the evolutionary hypothesis (macroevolution, not

---

[100] This section taken from: Heerin, Fred, *Show Me God. What The Message From Space Is Telling Us About God.* (Wheeling, IL: Searchlight Publications, 1995), pp. 268-271.

microevolution) is flawed, then there is really just one alternative. That is, God brought the universe into existence.

S: You have a point, I must admit.

B: Does it not make sense, then, due to what we have discussed thus far, to first consider the holy book that is right on the money as far as science goes? You see, according to my knowledge, the holy book of the Judeo-Christian faith is the only one that states that the universe began to exist.

S: I wouldn't know.

B: But if that is the case, does it not seem more prudent to consider Christianity in its message on salvation as opposed to other religions who are inaccurate on their scientific doctrines?

S: You got a point!

B: Should we pursue more of Leibniz now?

S: Sure. It's just interesting to see the philosophical and scientific confirmations parallel.

B: I agree. In any event, Gottfried Leibniz sought to answer the question why there was something instead of nothing by establishing a "Sufficient Reason" for it all (everything that exists must have a sufficient reason for its existence). Since nothing can occur, Leibniz believed, without a sufficient reason, there must exist a Being that transcends this world who Himself must be the Sufficient Reason for the things that exist. Pretty nifty, huh?

S: I remember Leibniz from my first college philosophy class. What was his thing on monads again?

B: Leibniz did not believe in atoms but rather explained that monads are what make up the world. These monads, he argued, are nonphysical and spiritual in nature. And, the *greatest monad* of all, of course, is the "Super Monad", which is what we call God.

S: Oh yes, I remember. I always thought that to be so strange. Now, you have already argued for God's existence based on morality, can you address William Soreley's moral argument?

B: This is a more complicated version. In a nutshell, he reasons that morality has its roots in God. Just as there is a natural order to the universe, so there is a moral order. This moral order dwells in personal agents who can will, or choose, to live morally. This is necessary for moral conduct to be possible. And just as the physical rings of Saturn are real, so is morality, although nonphysical. They are both part of the "furnitured warehouse" we call the universe. Moreover, it seems as though human beings, universally speaking, live according to some moral code.

S: According to, Soreley's view then, morality is objective and not relative.

B: Without a doubt. And God, according to Sorely, is the only rational source and explanation of these objective moral values.

S: But couldn't evolution have produced moral values?

B: If that is the case, then these values are not objective or absolute.

S: How so?

B: For the simple fact that they were *produced*. In other words, it has not always been the case that the act of rape is wrong, but rather this idea of wrongness was produced by evolution at a certain moment in time, which is really ethical relativism at best. In addition, imagine if evolution resulted in calling rape a moral act. Talk about hit-or-miss morality.

S: So what *if it was* produced by evolution?

B: Then we are really talking about *moral relativism,* which is a very troublesome system of moral thought.

S: How so?

B: You see, if relativism were true, the act of rape and torturing someone for the fun of it would not *really* be wrong.

S: Sure it is.

B: Why would it be?

S: Because it would not benefit the good of society.

B: Then we are really talking about societal *survival* and not necessarily what is really *good* or *bad*. Actions like murder, rape and innocent torture would be mere neutral ethical acts. And if you are correct, how are the acts of Hitler and mother Teresa different?

S: The answer seems obvious.

B: I agree, but the question is *why* is it obvious to you? Here the advocate of the moral argument would say that you are appealing to the moral law within you. And you seem to agree, just from arguing the way you do, that ethics is not illusory.

S: I *don't* think ethics is illusory.

B: Please then consider my argument,

> (1) If there is no God, then ethics is illusory
>
> (2) Ethics is not illusory
>
> (3) Therefore it cannot be the case that there is no God
>
> [4] Therefore God exists.

There is no good reason to affirm objective moral values unless there is an Objective Morality or *An Unchanging Moralitor*, so to say. It's simple, without a Lawgiver, there is no moral law, and if no moral law, as Dostoevski put it, then "all things are permitted." We'll get into this some more, I'm sure, when we deal with the problem of evil.

S: But that is crazy. "All things—permitted"?

B: I agree. But if God does not exist, then ethics is the result of mere human constructions. Humans who are the products of evolution. In turn, if this were true, morality would aim at survival, which has nothing to do with what is absolutely right or wrong.

S: I give up. This line of reasoning is foreign to me.

B: That is probably because you have not engaged in much of moral reasoning which, by the way, does not mean that one cannot live a moral life.

S: You're probably right.

B: You see, to argue *for* morality without the appeal to *metaethics*[101] makes the issue moot. When the nonbeliever says "one *ought to* do *this* and refrain from *that*" or "one *should* never commit *that* act but always *do this.*" He has entered into the realm of metaethics. Thus, to

---

[101] *Metaethics,* according to philosopher Milton D Hunnex "is the *study of moral statements* or *moral judgements* as contrasted with *normative ethics,* which is the study of *right and wrong or good and bad,* i.e., how behavior ought to be. Metaethics is concerned with the use of moral language and is *descriptive* and *analytical* rather than *prescriptive* and *substantive.*" See Hunnex, Milton D. *Chronological And Thematic Charts of Philosophers and Philosophies.* (Grand Rapids, MI: Academie Books, 1986), pg. 27.

be consistent, one cannot argue for morality without appealing to a Moral LawGiver—God—or else all is reduced to relativism and makes the issue moot.

S: It is starting make a little more sense. But this is pretty deep stuff, though very important I'm beginning to realize. But let me, then, ask you a few more questions.

B: Sure, go ahead.

S: Was it not Ruth Benedict, one of the foremost anthropologists in America who argued that "morality is merely conventional?"[102]

B: Yes it was, she defends moral relativism. She argues, "Conversely the most valued traits of our normal individuals have been looked upon in differently organized cultures as aberrant. Normality, in short, within a very wide range, is culturally defined."[103]

S: That's cultural relativism, isn't it?

---

[102] *Journal of General Psychology* 10 (1934): 59-82. Also see Beckwith, Francis J. *Do The Right Thing: A Philosophical Dialogue on the Moral and Social Issues of Our Time.* (Sudbury, MA: Jones and Barlett Publishers, 1996), pg. 5.

[103] Beckwith, Francis J. *Do the Right Thing: A Philosophical Dialogue on the Moral and Social Issues of Our Time.* (Sudbury, MA: Jones and Barlett Publishers, 1996), pg. 8

B: Certainly. She further says,

> We do not elevate it to the dignity of a first principle, we recognize that morality differs in every society, and is a convenient term for socially approved habits. Mankind has always preferred to say, "it is morally good", rather than "It is habitual", and the fact of this preference is a matter enough for critical science of ethics. But historically the two phrases are synonymous.[104]

S: What she says seems pretty clear, doesn't it, regardless of your previous points?

B: You still don't see the problem as clearly as I hoped you would. If morality is determined from culture to culture, than the extermination of the Jews during World War II was justified. After all, that was Nazian ethics. But we all *know* intuitively (and universally) that what was done to the Jewish people, and many others for that matter, was wrong, wicked, and cruel. The Nazis engaged in genocide in their attempt to systematically exterminate that part of the human race. Anyone who says otherwise is clearly morally handicapped. No doubt about it.

---

[104] *Ibid,*. pg. 8.

S: But is it not wrong for a culture to push their morality on another culture.

B: That is the *political correctness* of our culture—which obviously has not been thought through correctly. Think about it. If that was wrong, then other cultures should not have interceded on behalf of the Jews in Germany that were being exterminated.

S: This is what you were getting at earlier, right?

B: Yes.

S: But what about *our* culture? Is it not intolerant to push *your morality* down other people's throats? I mean, this is clearly wrong.

B: Is that your view of morality?

S: Yes it is.

B: How come you are pushing your morality on me right now?

S: It's self-refuting, huh?

B: It sure is. It's the argument from tolerance again. Some argue "it's wrong to judge. You should not judge." The obvious reply is "how come, then, you're judging me right now?" This is Logic 101.

S: Hmm.

B: Not only that, but tolerance presupposes disagreement.

S: What do you mean?

B: Well, you don't *tolerate* that which you *agree* with, do you?

S: I'm not following you.

B: The very notion of tolerance presupposes that one ought to tolerate that which one already disagrees with. Hence, one does not tolerate that which one agrees with.

S: In other words, if I asked you to be more tolerant of a certain sexual lifestyle's, and I myself claim to be tolerant of these sexual lifestyle's, then I am actually disagreeing with these lifestyle's, right?

B: That's exactly right. And this is because "tolerance" *presupposes* "disagreement."

S: I have to admit, that's very good. But let me ask you another question. Don't cultures differ on moral issues?

B: Once again, it does not follow from disagreement that moral truth does not exist. Entire cultures can be mistaken (NaziGermany) as can one individual. Secondly, as philosopher Francis Beckwith points out, ...sometimes-apparent moral differences are [not moral differences] at all but [factual differences]. During the Salem witch trial, certain individuals were put to death who were believed to be practicing witchcraft. We don't execute witches today, but not because our moral values have changed. We don't execute witches today because we don't believe that the practice of their craft has a fatal effect upon the community—contrary to what the residents of Massachusetts believed in the seventeenth-century.[105]

S: So, there's a factual difference as opposed to a moral difference?

---

[105] Beckwith, Francis J. *Politically Correct Death*. (Grand rapids, MI: Baker Books, 1993), pg. 21.

B: Granting this generalization, some argue that the people in India do not eat cows because of their belief in reincarnation. Eating the cow, they believe, is wrong because due to cycles of reincarnation the souls of previous living human beings may reside in the cow. But this is a *factual* difference, not a *moral* difference. You and I, for example, would agree that it is wrong, deeply immoral and wicked to have grandma (or the soul of grandma who inhabits the cow) for dinner, just as some people in India, but where we disagree is that we do not believe that grandma's soul resides in the cow. Hence, a factual difference.[106]

S: That clarifies it.

B: Moreover, it really overemphasizes moral differences and downplays similarities. C.S. Lewis, who taught Medieval and Renaissance literature at Cambridge University does say that sometimes there are different moralities, ...but these have never amounted to anything like a total difference. If anyone will take the trouble to compare the moral teaching of, say, the ancient Egyptians, Babylonians, Hindus, Chinese, Greeks and Romans, what will really strike him will be how very alike they are to each other and to our own.[107]

---

[106] *Ibid.,* pg. 22.
[107] Lewis, C.S. *Mere Christianity.* (New York: MacMillan Publishing Company, 1952), pg. 19.

S: That sounds about right too, I guess.

B: C.S. Lewis further argues,

> ...but for our present purpose I need only ask the reader to think what a totally different morality would mean. Think of a country where people were admired for running away in battle[108], or where a man felt proud of doublecrossing all the people who had been the kindest to him. You might just as well try to imagine a country where two and two makes five.[109]

S: That's funny.

B: Does it seem a bit more obvious now? It was James Rachel who said, regarding the Eskimos' value of human life concerning the making of certain choices that you and I normally do not face, "I emphasize this in order to show that the raw data of the anthropologists can be

---

[108] Some have argued that this does take place in some cultures. And somehow this is supposedly proof for moral relativism. I don't think so. If *lying* to your best friend or *doublecrossing* the person that has been the kindest to you are viewed as praiseworthy acts, then it seems that to tell the *truth* to your best friend or to be *honest* to the person that has been the kindest to you are viewed as vice. Thus, in such a culture, *lying* becomes a virtue and *truth telling* becomes vice. This is *not* moral relativism but a strange case of moral objectivism. Their objectivism is certainly warped, but it does affirm their notions of absolute virtues.

[109] Lewis. *Mere.*, pg. 19

misleading; it can make the differences in values between cultures greater than they are."[110]

S: All of this in defense of the moral argument, eh?

B: You bet. But it was worth the extra time, I would hold, since these are major moral issues and options infiltrating society, there is perhaps more to it than you imagine.

S: No, I am getting what you are saying. But what happens when moral absolutes conflict?

B: Then you go with the greater of the two and in doing so you are exempted from the lower one. Imagine, for example, an escaped convict on the prowl at night. He was convicted for murder and is obsessed with it. If he were to come to your door asking for your wife, who's upstairs sleeping, you are, according to graded absolutism[111], justified in not telling the truth to him (just like one does not owe an enemy in war the truth) in order to save your wife's life.

---

[110] Beckwith, *Politically Correct.*, pg. 22.

[111] This view holds that when moral absolutes conflict, it is one's duty to obey the higher of the two possible goods, and in doing so one is "exempted" (as Geisler puts it) from the lower of the two absolutes in conflict.

S: I see. So by obeying the higher of the two (saving my wife) by means of not telling the truth (to the murderer) I am *exempted* from the lower one (or "over-ride it") since it is a greater good[112] to preserve life than it is to tell the truth which would result in death. That seems plausible.

B: Give it some more thought, and we'll talk about it some other time. In any event, that is it for Soreley's moral argument.

S: You know, one argument that I never fully understood was what's his name? Anselm's argument from ontology.

B: Yes, there have been great minds throughout history on both sides of Anselm's ontological argument.

S: What is the form of the argument again?

B: Anselm argued that God is the greatest being that we as humans could ever conceive of. And since it is greater to exist in reality than to exist in the mind alone, God, being the greatest conceivable being, must thus exist.

---

[112] This view is know as *graded absolutism*. Here one chooses the greater of the two moral absolutes in conflict, and in doing so, by doing the greater good, one is *exempted* from the lower—hierarchical objectivism.

Furthermore, God exists not only in the mind but also in reality. Therefore, God must exist.

S: I still don't get that one.

B: Try to see if this makes more sense. A being whose nonexistence is inconceivable is greater than a being whose nonexistence is conceivable. But God is the greatest conceivable being there is. Thus, God's nonexistence must be inconceivable. Hence, God exists.[113]

S: Still, this one's a bit fuzzy for me.

B: Perhaps Plantinga's "Possible Worlds"[114] version helps. He begins with two definitions: (a) Maximal Excellence: To have omnipotence, omniscience, and moral perfection in *some* world. (b) Maximal Greatness: To have maximal excellence in *every* possible world. Then he states the argument,

(1) There is a possible world (w) in which there is a being (x) with maximal greatness.

(2) But (x) is maximally great only if (x) has maximal excellence in every possible world.

---

[113]Craig, *Reasonable Faith.*, pg. 79.

[114] Plantinga, Alvin C. *God, Freedom, and Evil.* (Grand Rapids, MI: Wm. B. Eerdmans Publishing Co., 1974), pp. 85- 112.

(3) Thus, (x) is maximally great only if (x) has omnipotence, omniscience, and moral perfection in every possible world.

(4) In (w), the proposition "There is no omnipotent, omniscient, and morally perfect being" would be impossible; that is, necessarily false.

(5) But what is impossible does not vary from world to world.

(6) Thus, the proposition "There is no omnipotent, omniscient, and morally perfect being is necessarily false in this actual world too.

Therefore,

(7) There actually exists in this world, and must exist in every possible world, an omnipotent, omniscient, and morally perfect being.

S: Very thought provoking. It helps a little bit.

B: I don't know how many times I read and re-read this argument for it to finally sink in. Its validity is clear, but some people question its soundness. It is certainly worth pondering.

S: Well, I'm ready to pass out. I better go to bed, but let me first get you a blanket in the closet.

B: Thank you!

S: Here you go.

B: Thanks again. You know, In case we don't wake up tomorrow, I want you to think about Pascal's Wager Argument before you close your eyes.

S: What's it about?

B: Pascal made the point that to live is a risk. Our very last breath can be five minutes away from now.

S: You got my attention.

B: Pascal said,

>   Either God is or he is not." But to which view shall we be inclined? Reason cannot decide this question. Infinite chaos separates us. At the far end of this infinite distance, a coin is being spun which will come down heads or tails. How will you wager? Reason cannot

make you choose either, reason cannot prove either wrong.[115]

S: I agree with that.

B: Good. Regarding bets, Thomas Morris points out that one should minimize ones losses and maximize ones gains.[116]

S: That is what my brother does at the racetrack.

B: But then Pascal goes deeper. He enters the metaphysical realm. Call it the metaphysical bet. He says, as I shared with you earlier, that by believing in God one has all to gain and nothing to lose[117]. If God does not exist, one has not really lost anything by believing in Him, except perhaps an immoral lifestyle, which one probably wouldn't need anyway. Moreover, by not believing[118] in God, there is a chance that

---

[115]Morris, *Making Sense.*, pg. 111.

[116]*Ibid.*

[117] Granted, it is a rather selfish argument.

[118] By believing in God (salvifically speaking) we do not mean "mere belief" but rather an acknowledgement of one's sense of wrongdoing (we have all missed the mark of perfection and are hence sinners in need of forgiveness regardless of how difficult and insulting this may be on our pride and ego). This salvation is given to us based upon God's grace and love (in him giving us His son who died on a Roman cross two thousand years ago for our wrong doings—of which if we do not acknowledge, salvation is impossible. This salvation of grace comes by "grace" through "faith" through "Christ" alone (Eph. 2:8, 9). One cannot work one's way into the kingdom of God as many are trying to

one will lose all that could have been gained (eternal life). So, if God exists and one believes in Him, then one has infinity to gain (heaven), and if He does not, one has not lost anything.

S: I understand your point.

B: But there is another point. You see, once the believer in God "checks out of here", if correct about his belief, he will know he was correct and gain eternal life. But if the nonbeliever is right, he will never have the satisfaction of knowing that he was correct. If he is wrong, he will suffer the consequences.

S: What if the believer is wrong?

B: He would never know it.

S: I have to admit, that is pretty good.

B: You see, for the theist, life does not end in a wooden casket. There is more to life than living and then becoming a fertilizer. At death the lonely nontheist, who rejects[119] belief in God, is

---

do. Our works are an insult to the finished works of Christ on the cross—who said "it is finished". That is, the work of salvation is completed—Jesus paid it all for you and me.

[119] Atheism derives from two Greek words "a" (meaning "non' or no") and "theos") meaning God. Thus. *a-theos*—no god belief or no godism. It is the willful rejection of belief in God. Now, some sophisticated

dressed up with nowhere to go. His destination or final stop is to become one with his grave trench, but what kind of hope is this?

S: Thanks for sharing that before we go to sleep. Hope or the lack of hope is not really the issue.

B: Certainly not, though an important factor for a happy and meaningful life.

S: Granted.

B: Atheism is really bankrupt as a system in that it has nothing to offer. At least nothing of quality and meaning. Like the famous atheist Bertrand Russell himself said, "Life is built on unyielded despair."

S: Thank you very *little*.

B: And, by the way, this is why atheism is bankrupt when it comes to providing hope.

---

atheists have tried to argue that atheism is "the absence of belief"—in God. But this is clearly confusing *agnosticism* (which says "I don't know") which atheism. This is because the atheist *knows* that outside of his limited real of thinking, it is possible that God exists (the atheist cannot logically assert that God does not exist based on facts). Thus, he has to admit that it is possible that God exists and that he (the atheist) does not *dogmatically know* that God does not exist. This seems more like agnosticism to me (but one thing the agnostic is sure of, or claims to know, is agnosticism.

There are not many, if any, atheists comforting sick children on the death beds in the hospitals. Only then is it theologically, or better `politically correct', to send in the pastors and the priests to give the sick and dying the *mythos*, right?

S: I get your point.

B: In any event, it's sort of the real issue once the arguments have been covered. Theists are not just after winning the argument, but want to see souls won into the Kingdom of God because the alternative is unspeakably horrifying.

S: I understand, and appreciate your passion.

B: All right then, where are you going to place your bet?

S: I'll have to think about it.

B: It was King David who said, "Man is like a breath; his days are like a fleeting shadow."[120]

S: There's truth to that, but I will have to ponder the issue some more.

---

[120] Psalm 144:4 (NIV)

B: Don't think too long. There really is not much
      to think about. As far as betting is concerned,
      the rational gambler would always bet on God.
      And you are rational, aren't you?

S: Good night.

Being unable to cure death, wretchedness and

ignorance,

men have decided, in order to live happy,

not to think about such things.

Blaise Pascal

At the Philosophers Pond

Chapter Four

B: What do you want to eat? It's on me?

S: No, no, no. I got it. Go ahead and order what you want.

B: Okay, you'll pay and I'll pray.

S: What do you want?

B: I think I'll take the Swedish garden omelet. What are you ordering?

S: I'm going for the big breakfast plate.

B: Hey, pretty good discussion last night!

S: Oh, I thought my head was going to fall off when we were finished with the theistic proofs. And on top of that, you just had to do the "wager thing." When I went to bed, I had to make sure I was *in* my bed and not in a trench.

B: [Laughter] It was just on my heart to share it with you, but you know, it *could* have happened and someday *will* happen, but I'm glad you're not in that trench.

S: Me too. But I have another issue I'd like to talk over with you.

B: What's that?

S: What I brought up to you the other day, the problems of evil in the world. How is it that God allows such evil?

B: What type of evil are you talking about?

S: Well, for example, look here in the *Chronicle* "Forty Dead Resulting From Earthquake." How could God allow that?

B: Are you saying that *natural events* are evil?

S: I guess nature is not evil *intrinsically* or in and of itself, but why did God let it happen.

B: Let's clarify that natural events are not evil. For example, if this earthquake occurred on an island that was completely uninhabited, we then would not call the earthquake evil. What really bothers you, and me I might add, is the *result,* of natural disasters. It's not the *events* themselves that are evil.

S: Good observation. But why is it that God allows such events to occur, not to mention the wicked things that men are doing to one another.

B: According to Judeo-Christianity, these events are the results of the fall of man.

S: You mean when the first human beings rebelled against God?

B: Yes.

S: Why should that affect us?

B: One answer is that the first man represented all of humanity, and just as the head of a nation decides the course of its history which affects his people, in like manner, the rebellion or sin of the first man has affected us. It may even be the case that if you or I were the first people on the scene, since human beings seem so alike, we would probably desire to do it "our way" too.

S: That seems ridiculous.

B: The issue is not whether it's ridiculous or not but whether it's true. It may seem ridiculous to you but it may still very well be true, right?

S: I suppose so. But what about all of the human evil we observe. Take, for example, Fyodor Dostoevsky's *The Brothers of Karamazov*. I have the book right here in my bag. Here we have the story of two brothers, Ivan—the atheist, and Aloysha—the believer. I think the words of Ivan are a deathblow to the existence of God. He says to his brother,

> By the way, a Bulgarian I met lately in Moscow...told me about the crimes committed by Turks and Circassians in all parts of Bulgaria through fear of a general rising of the Slavs. They burn villages, murder, outrage women and children, they nail prisoners by the ears to the fences, leave them so till morning, and in the morning they hang them—all sorts of things you can't imagine. People talk sometimes of bestial cruelty, but that's a great injustice and insult to the

beasts; a beast can never be so cruel as a man, so artistically cruel.[121]

Artistic cruelty is exactly the truth. Not to mention humans burning other humans in Nazi Germany. Just imagine the stench of burnt flesh passing over the homes in Europe as it fills the air night after night. In addition, premeditated starvation and human experimentation filled the camps. The stories of human evil never really seem to end.

B: I get your point and admit that I am as troubled as you are.

S: Let me finish, though. Ivan further describes,

The tiger only tears and gnaws, that's all he can do. He would never think of nailing people by the ears, even if he were able to do it. These Turks took pleasure in torturing children too; cutting the unborn child from the mother's womb, and tossing them up in the air and catching them on the points of their bayonets before their mother's eyes. Doing it before their mothers was what gave zest to the amusement.[122]

---

[121] Dostoevski, Fyodor. *The Brothers Karamazov.* (New York: Barnes & Noble Books, 1995), pg. 220.
[122] *Ibid.*

So artistically cruel is man.

B: Sounds like a 21st century abortion method to me.

S: I know, that's another great evil. Ivan finally says,

> Here is another scene that I thought very interesting. Imagine a trembling mother with her baby in her arms, a circle of invading Turks around her. They've planned a diversion; they pet the baby, laugh to make it laugh. They succeed, the baby laughs. At that moment a Turk points a pistol four inches from the baby's face. The baby laughs with glee, holds out its little hands to the pistol, and he pulls the trigger in the baby's face and blows out its brains. Artistic, wasn't it? By the way, Turks are particularly fond of sweet things they say.[123]

B: A horrifying picture to say the least. Dostoevsky certainly stated the problem of evil in concrete terms. But, before I attempt to share with you how I deal with this immense problem, let me ask you a question.

---

[123] *Ibid.*

S: What's that?

B: You sort of waver between atheism and agnosticism, don't you?

S: Something like that, yes!

B: What, according to your worldview, is evil?

S: What do you mean?

B: Well, granting the atheistic picture of the world, there can be no *real* evil.

S: Are you questioning my sincerity?

B: No. I know you are very serious about this issue, but just *what is evil* granting atheism?

S: I am not sure where you are going with this.

B: Well, for there to be such a thing as an *absolute evil*, there also has to be such a thing as an *absolute good*, at least it seems that way, for the problem to be taken seriously.

S: Okay, so what?

B: Who is this absolute good? *What* or *Who* is your point of reference? In other words, by whom or what authority or standard of right and wrong do you call certain things evil and other things good. After all, how does one debate between to opposite answers to such questions without an absolute standard of right and wrong (that must transcend ourselves)?

S: I don't know.

B: Is it you?

S: No. Nor is it you.

B: I was just going to say that. Who, then, is this absolute good? Who defines or tells us what *is* good and evil and so on?

S: Well, it certainly doesn't have to be God.

B: Oh yes, it certainly does. For one could not have an absolute evil without there being something that is absolutely good. And only by an appeal to this absolute Good could you and I call *this* or *that* evil. Now, in other words, we have a reference point. Thus, evil is actually indirect proof for the existence of God, if we are to take your question seriously.

S: I am not sure I understand you. In other words, are you saying that if the Ten Commandments are just the result of cultural religious traditions, then they're completely relative, but if they are from God, then God and his standard of right and wrong is the point of reference?

B: That's exactly what I am trying to get across to you. Now, let's look at a syllogism to make another point,

> (1) If atheism is true, then there is no such thing as an absolute evil
>
> (2) But there is such a thing as an absolute evil
>
> (3) Therefore, it cannot be the case that atheism is true
>
> (4) If atheism is not true, then God exists
>
> (5) Atheism is not true (2) and (3)
>
> (6) Therefore, God exists (4)

S: So, you actually think evil is *indirect proof* for God's existence?

B: Yes. And for you to have a point, you must *first* concede the theistic picture of the world. Thus, in affirming the existence of evil, you actually end up affirming, or better are borrowing, the theistic worldview to make your case. Let me share a few more syllogisms to make my point.

S: Let's see them.

B: All right, then. First,

(1) If there is no God, then moral notions are incoherent

(2) Moral notions are not incoherent

(3) Therefore, there is a God

Second,

(1) If objective moral values[124] exist (which you seem to imply in arguing against moral wickedness), then they must be grounded in God's very own being

---

[124] The belief that there are universal moral values *independent* and *transcendent* of man. Some things, are thus, *really right* and other things *really wrong*.

(2) Objective moral values do in fact exist (if they do not exist, then your argument from moral wickedness is illusory and relative, and if so, there's not an argument to be taken seriously)

(3) Therefore, God exists, and these objective moral values must be grounded in the nature of God; God's very own being

Thus,

(1) One cannot have a problem with evil unless one appeals to objective moral values (that must be grounded in God's being)

(2) You DO have a problem with evil (which is obvious since you are presently raising the argument)

(3) Therefore, you are appealing to objective moral laws that could only be grounded in God's very own being

(4) Therefore, God exists (and evil is one area of proof)

S: For the arguments to be sound[125] objective moral values or laws, of course, must be real.

B: Right, and this seems to be the case, at least from your point of view, since you raised the problem. Moreover, say for example that you have a problem with slavery and call it a wicked moral act of the past. If moral objectivism is false, then we could not improve our moral laws or things could not get any better precisely because morality would be relative. But this, of course (slavery being wrong and a thing of the past), is something that most of us would recognize and call a great evil and very unjust which could not be true *if* moral relativism were true. But if it is the case that such things are evil, then moral reform can indeed, and should, take place because there are some things that are ultimately morally wicked and other things that are objectively morally praiseworthy and true, regardless of time, culture or religious traditions.

S: Hmm? Well, I am certainly not going to drop my argument, so I guess you have a point.

B: A strong point indeed. J.P. Moreland said, in debating the atheist philosopher Kai Nielsen,

---

[125] the conclusion follows from true premises

> ...Christian theism helps explain the knowability of morality in a number of ways...Christian theism helps make sense out of how my moral faculties could have come about in the first place. How is it that humans can have institutional insight into the nature of morality? God has created us to know moral values.[126]

B: But furthermore, if moral objectivism was wrong, then, of course, all of the moral reformers, whom were absolutists, of the past would have to be wrong including Socrates, Aristotle, Jesus, Ghandi, and even Martin Luther King Jr. in his letter from the Birmingham jail.

S: Right, and this is what you alluded to earlier. Who in *this* day and age is qualified intellectually to get up against these moral and very thoughtful *heavyweights* of the past? Most people don't even know the capitols of their neighboring countries, much less do they have a robust case for their views on morality. It's pathetic.

B: Good point. And, once again, I too take the existence of moral evil seriously. But, of course,

---

[126] Moreland, J.P. and Kai Nielsen, *Does God Exist? The Debate Between Theists & Atheists.* (Amherst, N.Y.: Prometheus Books, 1993), pg.119.

it boils down to which world view can best account for this evil; which system of thought is more plausible in its explanation for it, and where lies the solution, and if no fully satisfactory solution, what "probable" and "logically possible" solution, then, can be offered?

S: Very clever.

B: I am ready to move on as long as you admit that for your first argument to have *any* validity you are *borrowing* concepts that could only come from my world view, thus you are assuming my philosophy while trying to refute it. This is clearly another point for my camp. If you disagree, then your argument is *not* grounded in any substance since your worldview does not contain nor can it account for such evil by definition. The bottom line is that there can be no moral law if there is no Moral LawGiver. Without there being a Moral Law Giver, morality is once again reduced to mere relative conventions. But since there are moral laws, there must also be a Moral LawGiver.

S: I'll buy your point. I am not willing to argue against that because, as you said earlier, if I do, I'd have to say that the acts of NaziGermany and Apartheid, etc. are morally neutral acts and ideologies which is a world view I am not willing to defend.

B: You are more *intellectually honest* than I thought.

S: Please, don't start that stuff again. Now, don't you think there is an inconsistency between the existence of a good God and evil. For the two to co-exist seems rather implausible. I mean, consider my argument,

> *(1) If* God exists, then, as you believe
> (2) God is good
> (3) God is loving
> (4) God is omnipotent (all-powerful)
> (5) God is omniscient (all-knowing)
> (6) Evil exists
> (7) God and evil cannot co-exist
> Therefore,
> (8) *It seems* that God does not exist

B: But I would question premise eight, that *God and evil cannot co-exist.* I am of the view that God gave man free will. I, of course, could be wrong here, but it seems *more plausible* that man has some sort of free will than not. I would agree with C.S. Lewis who believed that one cannot separate genuine love and human freedom. Plantinga, I think, has a solution here.

S: Before we get into his argument, as it relates to free will, couldn't God have made us make better choices?

B: First, if God removed or did not grant us free will, then we would be the robotic inhabitants of a world doing whatever we were commanded to do. None of our actions would have any sincerity. Thus, if God commanded 'X', we would perform 'X', not based on any freedom whatsoever, but of necessity. In such a world, if God left up to us, responding to His call of offering us a wonderful plan of salvation with such great promises, how would He truly *know* that we desire to have a relationship with Him.

S: I guess He wouldn't. It would be a very insincere relationship, if one could even call it a relationship.

B: Moreover, if he made or forced us to *make* certain choices, we really would not be choosing at all, would we? In other words, what we'd choose would really *not* be *our* choosing.

S: I guess not.

B: If God would have created us that way, that would *not* have been the best possible world[127]. It is a *better possible world* where the beings contained in it possess free will. In addition, it is likely that *this* world contains *less* amount of evil *than any other possible world* God could have created while maintaining free will. This, we can argue, is the best possible world, granting human freedom (and our finite understanding of the nature of things, especially as it relates to free will, etc.). As Plantinga[128] put it,

> A world containing creatures who are sometimes significantly free (and freely perform more good than evil actions) is more valuable, all else being equal, than a world containing no free creatures at all. Now God can create free creatures, but he cannot *cause* or *determine* them to do only what is right. For if he does so,

---

[127] the way things could have been like; a possible state of affairs

[128] This is known as the *Free Will Defense* Accordingly, it is logically possible for God to co-exist with evil. Plantinga, argues that it is possible for God to create a world containing free moral agents who freely chose to do the wrong thing (evil). Thus, in this respect, it seems foolish to require of God's omnipotence, when creating the world, the existence of free moral agents while not having the capacity of committing evil (as a result of free will). Thus, according to Plantinga, though God is truly omnipotent, it is still not within his capacity to bring about a world that contains the good (the moral good) but not the capacity of the occurrence of evil. See Plantinga's *God, Freedom and Evil*.

> then they are not significantly free after all; they do not do what is right *freely*. [129]

S: That makes sense.

B: I think so.

S: Is this the philosopher that is so highly respected today?

B: Yes, Plantinga has done a lot of good work in areas of both philosophy and theology. But, to get back to what we were talking about, Plantinga further reasons,

> To create creatures capable of *moral good*, therefore, he must create creatures capable of moral evil; and he cannot leave these creatures *free* to perform evil and at the same time prevent them from doing so. God did in fact create significantly free creatures; but some of them went [**wrong in the exercise of their freedom**]: this is the source of moral evil. The fact that these free creatures sometimes go wrong, however, counts neither against God's omnipotence nor against his goodness; for he could have forestalled the occurrence of moral evil

---

[129] Plantinga, Alvin, *The Nature of Necessity*. (Oxford: Clarendon Press, 1974), pp. 165-167.

only by exercising the possibility of moral good.[130] [my emphasis]

S: That seems to be a good explanation.

B: I think so. In addition, regarding free will and genuine love, A.E. Wilder-Smith says,

> Without this freedom, true love is impossible...if love is replaced by force, then the possibility of real love is abolished...Absolute free will, then, is a prerequisite of all true love.[131]

Moreover, he reasons,

> Love is only satisfied when returned free-willed love is won. God is not constrained in any way to love us, but just loves us because He is love. Such divine love does not force us to return His love. The very attempt to do so would destroy the basis of real love and all real virtue...Because God, being love, decided to create the impossibility of true love among men [mankind], He had to take the chance that His intended partners [by means of having a

---

[130] *Ibid.*

[131] Wilder-Smith, *Why Does God Allow It?* (Costa Mesa, CA: TWFT Publishers, 1980), pp. 22-23

relationship with God] in love would not love Him at all.[132]

Finally Wilder-Smith concludes,

> God's eternal plan is to set up a kingdom of real love on earth and in heaven. But reaching this end involves a built-in risk—that of hate [by not choosing the good, one automatically chooses the bad] and vice arising instead of love and virtue.[133]

S: I see no problem with either of these points.

B: I think they're plausible. Without this freedom, there would be no such thing as moral responsibility or moral actions.[134]

S: But I have another problem. Since God created everything, didn't God also, create evil?

B: No. I think you are confusing some terms. You see, evil is to be sure, "something" but it is not some "thing." If we put it in standard form, what you are saying looks like this,

---

[132] *Ibid.*, pg. 25.

[133] *Ibid.*

[134] Moreland, J.P. and Nielsen, Kai. *Does God Exist.*, pg. 115

(1) God created everything

(2) Evil is something

(3) Therefore, God created evil

The major premise is what is in question. As I said, I believe that evil is "something" but it is *not* some tangible "thing" that God created.

S: So evil is nonphysical?

B: Right. So that argument is flawed.

S: What, then, is evil?

B: Christian thinkers have differed on a precise definition throughout history. Augustine, for instance, maintained that evil is the *lack of goodness* in a thing. A tree with a *rotten* spot Augustine believed to be the opposite of what is a natural and healthy tree. In like manner, as it relates to humans and an evil will, by not choosing the right thing, one automatically chooses the wrong thing. This is evil.

S: What have others said?

B: Well, we don't have the time to sit here till the cows come home. But Christian philosopher Douglas Geivett has developed one definition that I like. He argues that evil is the departure from the way things ought to be.[135]

S: What ought things to be like? I mean if I lose a leg due to natural evil— I'm sorry, I meant to say "natural disaster"—this is clearly not the way things ought to be.

B: Those are questions Geivett raises. If we combine some of the issues that he raises and tie it into an argument, I think we have a good grasp of what evil is and where it leads us,

> (1) What is good in a world made out of chance (granting the evolutionary hypothesis)?
> (2) What could be broken in such a world?
> (3) What could be repaired in a world of evolution? (Ought things to be a certain way without a plan or design?)
> (4) If there is no designer (God) then language like "things ought to be like this or that" becomes meaningless
> (5) Nothing, really, could be broken in such a world and hence nothing needs to be repaired if no designer (God) exists

---

[135] Geivett, Douglas. "The Problem of Evil." Lecture. Apologetics 2, Simon Greenleaf University. Anaheim, CA, June 6, 1996. Geivett is also professor of philosophy at Talbot School of Theology at Biola University, La Mirada, CA.

(6) Only if there is a designer can things be broken. Only if there is a designer could one complain that the loss of a leg or an arm is the way things ought *not* to be

(7) If God, then, does not exist, then neither does evil (as we also saw before)

(8) If God (the designer) does exist, then one can say that "things ought not to be *this* way, but that way" since they were designed accordingly.

(9) This type of evil, if we can call it such, does exist

Therefore,

(10) God exists.

S: Now THAT'S a good argument.

B: I like it.

S: It certainly carries a lot of weight.

B: It's a deathblow to atheism, I think.

S: But couldn't one argue that the theistic explanation for the existence of evil is perhaps not a logical problem, as we came to agreement before, but rather that it is highly implausible.[136]

---

[136] This is known as the *evidential problem of evil.*

B: I guess one could, and frankly I do think that you have a point here. However, it's the *totality of arguments* in *support of theism* that make theism *the most plausible* worldview, I would say.

S: Right, all the stuff we discussed before. But, why doesn't God do away with all evil right now? You theists, if anybody, should know why.

B: Seriously, why is that? Plantinga makes a good point here, "Why suppose that if God does have a good reason for permitting evil, the theist would be the first to know?"[137]

S: Go on.

B: He further reasons,

> Perhaps God has a good reason, but that reason is too complicated for us to understand. Or perhaps He has not revealed it for some other reason. The fact that the theist doesn't know why God permits evil is, perhaps, an interesting fact about the theist, but by

---

[137] Plantinga, *God, Freedom and Evil,*. pg. 10.

itself it shows little or nothing of the rationality of belief in God.[138]

Thus, the atheist must have more ammunition than that. Plantinga finally says, "Much more is needed for the atheological argument even to get off the ground."[139]

S: Fair enough.

B: Moreover, if God did do away with evil right away, what would happen to you and me?

S: I guess we'd be done away with as well?

B: That's right. We would be a part of history a microsecond ago. So God is awfully patient with man, don't you think?

S: I suppose so.

B: What do you mean "I suppose so?"

S: No, you're right, if He exists, we certainly have a patient and long suffering God. But I still wish, if He exists, that He'd *somehow* do away with evil.

---

[138] *Ibid.*
[139] *Ibid.*

B: He will.   You see, according to Christian theism, evil is a *temporal issue*. It will be done away with someday. From a Christian point of view, I think, the philosopher Peter Kreeft and Ronald K. Tacelli do a great job in summing up the problem of evil. Regarding the origin and nature of evil, they state:

> ➤ The nature of spiritual evil is sin, separating ourselves from God.
> ➤ The origin of spiritual evil is human free will.
> ➤ The end for which God allows spiritual evil is to preserve human free will, that is, human nature.
> ➤ The nature of our physical evil is suffering.
> ➤ The origin of physical evil is spiritual evil [since moral evil brought about natural evil]. We suffer because we sin.
> ➤ The end or use of physical evil is spiritual discipline and training for our own ultimate perfection and eternal joy. (It is also just punishment for sin and a deterrence from sin.)[140]

S: I see.

B: And, of course, when those who are His (those who have accepted God's gift of salvation by means of accepting His Son who died for the sins of humanity) exit "out-of-here", there will be no more such evil. But it should also be mentioned that natural evil such as disease and suffering could draw us closer to God. For example, take a person lying on the deathbed. He has been so busy in his pursuit of worldly

---

[140] Kreeft, *Handbook,*. pg. 142

goods and has never really sat down to ponder life after death seriously. Suppose he got in a boat accident while water skiing and ended up in the hospital. For the first time, this man finds himself in an immovable position. For the first time does he realize how close to death he was out there on the lake that afternoon. Somehow, after doing a lot of thinking and reflecting back on his life, he comes to his senses and says "yes" to God after conversing with a minister. If these were not the circumstances, he may never have realized that his life is but a vapor.

S: So, from a Christian vantage point, evil is not gratuitous, right?

B: That's right.

S: But what about the wicked acts of religious people throughout history? I mean, not only is history filled with religious wars and great evils, but in the case of the Old Testament, God commanded the Israelites to wipe out numerous communities. How do you explain this? Is there a good answer?

B: You know, Sixten. This is something that many people struggle with. But if one does his homework, one will discover that there is more to the historical context. In other words, there is much more that needs to be mentioned to get the story straight. First, many people can *claim* to be Christians while they are not. Can't they?

S: Sure they can.

B: So to claim to be a Christian does not necessarily make you a Christian anymore than I would become a Toyota pick-up truck if I sat in a garage for a week, right?

S: [Laughter] I follow you.

B: In addition, the horrible acts committed by such proclaiming believers in Christianity cannot be traced down to the teachings of their founder— Jesus Christ. Furthermore, Jesus himself said that many people would come in *his* name doing many things that he did *not* command. Thus, he foretold of such hypocrites. And this is, of course, also a fulfillment of prophecy.

S: I guess the same would be true of most religions.

B: Yes, except for those religions that advocate violence if one does not become a follower of their religion. Now, these communities you referred to in Old Testament times were very wicked people. They committed all sorts of crime. These people, whom God were angry with, engaged in human sacrifice, unnatural sexual acts, rape and other abhorrent behavior. They were much like "the predator's of the desert." The worst gang-members you've ever seen. Imagine these people ruling the streets of Los Angeles, would it be fair to bring in the national guard – whether we as a people, or God as the author of life, commanded us to put such "cancer of moral depravity"[141] to end by means of the most radical surgery? In addition, the behavior of these people and their cruel and unusual religious rituals were a threat to the survival of the Israelite's whom God had set apart to be an example of His people to the rest of the world. God did not want His people to get corrupted.

S: Hmm… That clarifies it a bit. You know, Benjamin, you have really made me think about a lot of issues.

B: I hope so. After all, there really are *knowable truths to pursue,* and what strikes me different with you is that you are not like most of my unbelieving friends. They frankly do not even want to talk about *anything* as it relates to *ultimate issues.* To them if one says one has discovered the truth, this is the equivalent of discovering a new "thing" or hobby like jet skiing or parachute jumping.

---

[141] Archer, Gleason L. *Encyclopedia of Bible Difficulties.* Grand Rapids, MI: Zondervan Publishing

S: What lies behind that line of reasoning?

B: I don't know, but it surely is the height of human folly. But what about *you*?

S: I'll have to think about it some more.

B: Don't think about too long, today or tomorrow could be *your* last day. The death rate, after all, is 100%. You can be *sure* that we are all going to make it, sooner or later.

S: I know. And to be honest, I am a bit uncomfortable with my position.

B: I hope you come to your senses soon.

S: It's good to see you again.

B: You too.

S: I tell you what, though. I would like to talk about a few more issues.

B: We'll talk again soon, I have a plane to catch tomorrow morning and have to finalize a speech I have been asked to give on the issue of God and Evil. I will be back next week, let's meet again and see if we can make sense out of your other questions?

S: That sounds great.

B: But don't be deceived, if my plane goes down, I know where I'm going. Do you, if something goes wrong before we meet again?

S: No, I don't.

B: By now you know far more about these issues than the average believer in God, this puzzles me.

S: I know. It puzzles me too.

For God so loved the world

that He gave His only begotten Son,

that whoever believes in Him

should not perish

but have everlasting life.

Jesus Christ